No. D343642   Class 720.9424

Author MORIARTY

Title Buildings of the Cotswolds

Buildings of the Cotswolds

DENIS MORIARTY Buildings

of the Cotswolds

LONDON
VICTOR GOLLANCZ LTD
in association with
PETER CRAWLEY
1989

Dedication

For my parents
May and Patrick
with my love

edited by Denis Moriarty

Alec Clifton-Taylor's
BUILDINGS OF DELIGHT

First published in Great Britain 1989
in association with Peter Crawley
by Victor Gollancz Ltd
14 Henrietta Street, London WC2E 8QJ

British Library Cataloguing in Publication Data
Moriarty, Denis
 Buildings of the Cotswolds.
  1. England. Cotswolds. Buildings of historical
 importance. Architectural features
  I. Title   II. Clifton-Taylor, Alec, *1907–1985*
 720′.9424′17
  ISBN 0-575-04059-9

Maps drawn by John Craig
Photoset in Great Britain by
Rowland Phototypesetting Ltd, Bury St Edmunds, Suffolk
Printed and bound in Great Britain by
Butler and Tanner Ltd, Frome, Somerset

Contents

Acknowledgements

During much travelling and in the writing of this book I have been extremely conscious of the help I have had from numerous people.

First from Philip Burkett, who has generously allowed me the guidance of the notes about Cotswold buildings made by the late Alec Clifton-Taylor, with whom I worked on BBC TV's *Six English Towns* series, and to whom I owe the greatest debt of all. I am also enormously grateful to Professor Jack Simmons and to Anthony Turner, both of whom generously read the text at a crucial stage and offered much helpful guidance, which I gladly accepted.

In the course of many journeys, I have been given much help by Cotswold residents, parish priests, custodians, caretakers and local government officials, all of whom I would have liked to have named personally, had that been possible. My friends, as ever, have put houses and hospitality at my disposal and I am particularly grateful to Noreen and James Grout and to Joan Crawley. Anne Jenkins has again worked with quicksilver efficiency in converting my wayward manuscript into a presentable typescript.

My family – my parents, my wife Brigid and our children Joshua, Edmund, Eleanor and Tristan – have been wonderfully supportive, uncomplainingly bearing the burden of the day – largely around dawn but stretching also to well past midnight. They have given me tremendous encouragement for which no words of thanks are really adequate.

Finally, I have to thank that happy and efficient team at Gollancz for much enjoyable collaboration and in particular my publisher, Peter Crawley, who has encouraged me editorially as well as illustratively – and I hope his keen-eyed photographs, original to this book, will excite readers to see things afresh which might otherwise have gone unnoticed.

Denis Moriarty
London March 1989

Introduction

THIS BOOK is about the buildings of the Cotswolds, perhaps the most attractive, popular and homogeneous region, in architectural terms, in Britain; it is concerned in particular with characteristic buildings of all types that have given me especial pleasure. They are, for the most part, readily accessible: churches, manor houses and farms, town and village architecture, and great houses open to the public or where, at least, their exteriors can be glimpsed.

There are nine small towns in the Cotswolds which have large numbers of outstanding buildings – Burford, Chipping Campden, Cirencester, Malmesbury, Minchinhampton, Painswick, Tetbury, Winchcombe and Witney – and most of them should be visited at least once. They have dictated the alphabetical arrangement of this book, and from whatever direction you approach, it is worthwhile looking at a detailed road map (the Ordnance Survey references to each entry are given as a quick guide) and noting other places on the way that should on no account be missed.

The choice of buildings is selective, and necessarily subjective, and has its roots in the unpublished notes of the late Alec Clifton-Taylor. With him I made a number of journeys through the Cotswolds during our collaboration when I was his producer of the series of *English Towns* which he wrote and presented for BBC television. I am most grateful to Christopher Burkett (and his father Philip) in whose hands the copyright now resides, for giving me access to this store of lively and enlightening material. *Buildings of the Cotswolds* is, therefore, intended for the public whose interest in buildings was stimulated by those television programmes and who, I hope, will enjoy an overall guide to them. Those who want to take a more detailed interest should consult David Verey's indispensable volume *Gloucestershire: The Cotswolds* in the Buildings of England series. A more lyrical view of the Cotswold scene is given in Susan Hill's *Spirit of the Cotswolds*, and Alec Clifton-Taylor's *The Pattern of English Building* (revised Jack Simmons, 1987) is a finely written work about traditional building materials, and makes special reference to Cotswold stone.

The Cotswolds lie almost entirely on limestone, a swathe of natural building stone which stretches from Portland Bill in the south-west and runs, broadly speaking, in a north-easterly direction through Gloucestershire, Warwickshire, Northamptonshire and Lincolnshire to the River Humber and beyond. The boundaries of the Cotswolds are somewhat arbitrary, but the north-western limit, an escarpment rising in places to over 1,000 feet with glorious views overlooking the Vale of Evesham and across to the Malvern Hills, is clearly defined. Elsewhere it is not so easy; the Cotswolds embrace a sizeable part of Gloucestershire, a substantial area of Wiltshire, a corner of Worcestershire (who could doubt that Broadway, even below the ridge, was of the Cotswolds?) the north-western edge of Oxfordshire, and the southern fringe of Warwickshire.

Within this area there is a wealth of good building which has survived, relatively unscathed, the pressures of the twentieth century. The towns are probably most at risk, but Cirencester, Chipping Campden, Minchinhampton, Painswick, Tetbury and Burford can still lay claim to be among the finest in their league in the country. The villages – too self-conscious, some may say perhaps out of envy – have fared remarkably well, and places like Bourton-on-the-Water, Broadway, Bibury, Barnsley, Castle Combe, Stanton, the Slaughters and Swells must be amongst the showpieces of the kingdom.

The landscape provides infinite variety. It is well watered; streams, crossed by splash ford and rustic bridge, glide gently down to join the Rivers Churn and Windrush, and then on to the River Thames above Oxford. Wide vistas open up above Broadway, views stretch for miles from the churchyard at Saintbury (**161**); manor houses at Owlpen (**146**) and Ozleworth nestle in secluded combes, while on top among lonely windswept uplands, there are only flocks of sheep for company. These pastures have been full of sheep since the Middle Ages. People grew rich on wool, and on the proceeds they built themselves churches, farms and houses. They had the cash, and they had the stone.

The limestone is plentiful, readily available and easily worked, and it provides the clue to the Cotswolds, and gives the area its extraordinary unity. Nearly every village had its own quarry, and from some, Guiting, Taynton, Barrington and Painswick, to name only four, the stone was of such repute that it travelled far afield. Nor does the stone lack variety, sometimes a creamy yellow colour, or a delicate grey, and in the marlstone region on the Oxfordshire –Warwickshire border, an attractive tawny brown. The stone comes also in different shapes and sizes: blocks of ashlar, mainly, but not exclusively, to be seen on churches and the more substantial houses and farms, and rubblestone, more often used for the smaller domestic buildings and walls in the fields.

The crowning glory is the stone roof, clad in what is confusingly referred to as 'stone slates', and seen in profusion, even on the most modest cottage. Stonesfield in Oxfordshire was the best-known quarry, though there was a whole range of others yielding such slates not far from Stow-on-the-Wold. The Cotswold roof, a work of great artistry and skill, is one of the sights of England. The limestone, the right material in the right place, is the reason why everything can still look so good in the Cotswolds; the architecture and the landscape are as one.

The characteristic architectural landmarks of the Cotswolds are the Perpendicular churches with their stately towers, and the manor houses. Of the churches, Northleach (**141**), Chipping Campden (**63**), and Cirencester (**70**) are among the outstanding examples. The limestone is often of such fine quality that it provided craftsmen with the opportunity to create exquisite carving in window tracery, parapets, canopies, such as at Meysey Hampton and Bampton, whole porches, as at Cirencester (**73**) and Northleach (**141**), and an abundance of gargoyles and monsters. Adderbury, Aldsworth, Bloxham, Fairford, Elkstone (**105**) have them in terrifying array.

The manor houses, often built by prosperous clothiers, grey-gabled and at their best with clipped yew for company, are quintessential Cotswolds. Nearly every village and hamlet seems to have one, but if a selection has to be made Ablington (**12**), Nether Lypiatt (**32**), Medford House (**132**), Bibury Court (**30**), Kelmscott, Owlpen (**146**), Poulton (**154**) and Upper Slaughter should be high on every shortlist. Frequently in a village it is the group that provides the focus rather than any one particular building, and such is this cumulative impact that it is easy to miss the elegant ashlar and the adornments, the refinements of finials, gate-posts, balls and urns. The eye for detail will always be rewarded.

It could be argued that because they were made of stone, Cotswold buildings have survived better than their counterparts elsewhere of timber and brick, and indeed a whole range of historic building types is on show. There are castles, Broughton (**41**), a particularly beautiful and ancient family home, Sudeley, Beverston (**26**), and splendid town houses, particularly in Cirencester (**83**), Burford (**46**) and Painswick (**153**). A characteristic focus of the towns is the market hall; Tetbury, Dursley (**101**) or Witney (**200**) are good examples, and the market crosses at Malmesbury and Castle Combe (**53**) rank among the best of their kind. There are also impressive rectories at Bishop's Cleeve, Buckland and Kingham (**123**), reminders of days when a parson's freehold was substantial and even a man of God could be a man of property (at least for the duration of an incumbency), a powerful incentive for a long stay in the parish. Burford did itself especially proud, with a rectory (**46**) *and* a vicarage (**47**). For the less fortunate, Chipping Campden, Chipping Norton (**62, 69**) and Wotton-under-Edge all have almshouses of considerable distinction.

The rivers and streams have many crossings, and the water-level bridges, at Bourton-on-the-Water and Lower Slaughter (**169**), and the old bridge over the Coln at Bibury, suit their locations to perfection. Farm houses and farm buildings abound, and the gabled dovecot is a familiar sight. The dovecot interiors are of great interest, and at Minster Lovell, Chastleton and Elkstone (**107**), an unusual example, it is possible to sample something of the dove's-eye-view. Cotswold barns are legion and legendary; fine groups are to be seen at Ablington, Southrop and Cogges and at Kelmscott where William Morris had the manor.

Archaeologically, too, the Cotswolds have much to offer. There are important Roman sites at Chedworth and Woodchester (the latter only rarely on view), and the Corinium Museum at Cirencester has some excellent mosaics. There is impressive Saxon work, in the churches at Daglingworth (**90/1**) and Langford, and a wealth of Romanesque, the most compelling of which is to be seen at Quenington, Windrush (**195**), Elkstone (**105**), and Malmesbury, where the south porch of the abbey is of international importance (**129**). The fonts at Southrop, Burford (**50**) and Rendcomb should on no account be missed.

Some churches show interesting wall painting, especially at St Nicholas, Oddington, and Burton Dassett (**52**). The stained glass at Fairford is justly famous (**111**), and there are some fine brasses, notably at Northleach and Chipping Campden. The Cotswolds are rich in church monuments; some of the most extraordinary are to be seen at Badminton, Swinbrook (**179**) and Meysey Hampton (**131**), and the churchyard topiary and tomb-chests at Painswick (**151**) have no equal anywhere in the country. The churches are nearly always worth a visit. They are invariably beautifully cared for, surrounded by well-kept graveyards, and fortunately and nowadays unusually, *Deo gratias*, often unlocked.

The Cotswolds escaped the Industrial Revolution, except at Witney and at Chipping Norton (**69**) in Oxfordshire, and near Stroud in the valley of the River Frome. A canal was built linking the Thames and the Severn which has left a romantic architectural legacy at the tunnel near Coates, and there were two main railway lines with cross-country branches. There was, however, no mass movement of materials, which elsewhere in the country did much to distort the traditional building pattern. The Victorians, it is true, laid a heavy hand on many a suffering parish church, but some splendid ashlar stone provided G. E. Street with perhaps his best-ever chance at Toddington (**188**). Here also, Charles Hanbury-Tracey produced a skilful Gothick at the Manor (**187**). G. F. Bodley's work is seen to good effect at All Saints, Selsey.

It was fortunate, and entirely appropriate, that the Cotswolds always attracted some of the leading exponents of craft and design. Following in the footsteps of William Morris, who first encouraged an aesthetic appreciation of the region from Kelmscott, C. R. Ashbee established his Guild of Handicrafts at the beginning of this century in Chipping Campden, where F. L. Griggs and others later founded the Campden Trust. Ernest Gimson and the Barnsley brothers, designers in the best tradition of the Arts and Crafts, worked from Sapperton. More recently, and not before time, local authority planning departments have responded to local representation by insisting, for the most part, on sensitive siting of new building and the use of consonant materials.

The Cotswolds are hugely enjoyable. This is an area to visit again and again. 'If I wanted to introduce a friend to English traditional architecture at its most *succulent*,' said Alec Clifton-Taylor in his introduction to his television programme on Cirencester, 'it is to the Cotswolds I would turn before anywhere else.'

Denis Moriarty, London 1989.

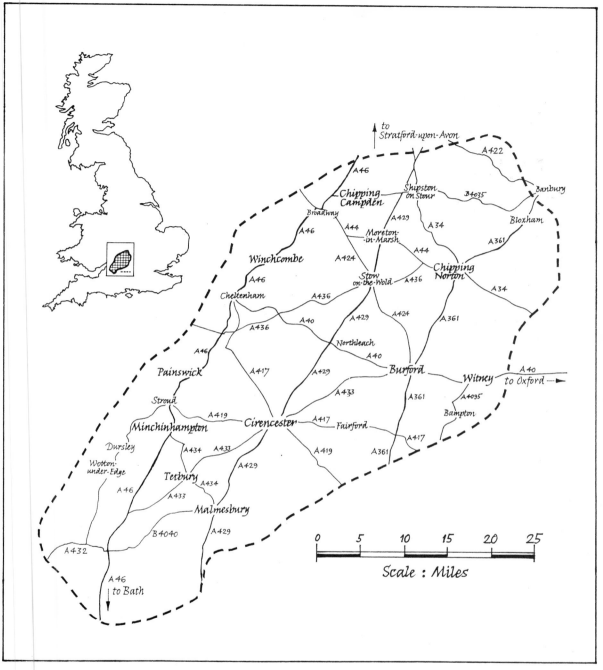

Outline map of the Cotswolds. This only shows major routes and a fraction of the places mentioned in the text. It is essential that a fully-detailed 4 miles to 1 inch road atlas should be used in conjunction with this map.

A map reference accompanies each entry. This relates to the Ordnance Survey 1:50,000 first, second and Landrover series; first to the number of the sheet, and then a six-figure reference, eastings and northings in the prescribed manner.

Ablington

GLOUCESTERSHIRE
OS 163 107077
9 miles north-east of Cirencester

◁ Ablington House,
Bibury

THERE COULD BE no better place to start. Ablington is secret and remote, no more than a hamlet taking shelter in the valley of the River Coln, a quiet stream which rises on the ridge above Cheltenham and, twenty miles to the south-east as the crow is supposed to fly, drains into the Thames at Lechlade. The village is entirely unspoiled.

The Manor House, dated 1590, hides discreetly behind a high wall. It has three bays with gables, and the porch with the inscription *Plead thou my cause O Lord* is its most attractive feature. It was the home of Arthur Gibbs, author of *A Cotteswold Village*, originally published in 1898, a charming and useful historical account of life in this heavenly part of England before the turmoils of the First World War. The house preserves its roughcast, a rendering of sand, gravel and stone chippings which may well be contemporary with the original building. On rubblestone houses of the Cotswolds roughcast was once commonly used, and if it hides a rather coarse stone and blends with the natural limestone colour, it can look quite successful. Roughcast has long fallen into disuse, either because it became less fashionable and people were no longer shy about showing their rubblestone, or because improvements in masonry technique made the use of rubblestone more effective against the damp and draught which roughcast was intended to ward off.

Ablington House (**12**) is a sizeable mid-seventeenth-century farmhouse, faithfully restored about 1920 when it acquired gateposts and guardian lions, carved in stone, which came from the Houses of Parliament. The beautifully tended yews make a fine entrance, and this house provides a handsome introduction to the village from the south. There are other attractive houses and cottages, but no church, although opposite Ablington Manor is a barn, complete with transepts or 'streys'. It is larger than most churches, and even resembles one; clearly, just to be in Ablington is spiritual uplift enough.

Adderbury

OXFORDSHIRE
OS 151 472354
3½ miles south-east of Banbury

ADDERBURY HAS GROWN from the marlstone, a Middle Lias limestone rich in iron, tawny brown in colour and much in evidence in this part of Oxfordshire and in south-east Warwickshire. There are really two villages, each with its own manor house and green divided by the Sor Brook, a stream that rises around Tysoe in Warwickshire. Adderbury is again disrupted (and indeed bombarded) to the east by murderous traffic thundering up the A423 between Oxford and Banbury. It leaves Adderbury House, now a home for the elderly but once the grandest house in the village, set in a park stranded on the far side of the busy main road. In no circumstances is this a good arrangement.

A quiet lane leads to the church, and here lies much of the interest. To the south is the Old Vicarage, the best of the houses, with an early Georgian front, and the Manor House, stone but with a brick chimney. To the north is the Grange and the tithe barn, a friendly old building of the Middle Ages. Unfortunately machine-made tiles on one side, and the dormer windows and glazing slightly spoil the effect. Thatch makes a welcome appearance, and down by the mill is a leafy walk, muddy (and worse) to the shoes as it serves as an 'exercise' run for dogs.

The church of St Mary, Early English cruciform when it was built, was enlarged in the fourteenth century and has close similarities with the church of the same dedication at Bloxham, two and a half miles to the west. The colour of the stone is golden brown and partly grey. The exterior is rich, particularly that of the chancel, with its tall windows of the early fifteenth century. To the north is a vestry with a lovely oriel window, apparently Tudor, facing east. The friezes of grotesques just below the parapets around the aisle are superb. The large figures to the north and east are especially fine, with birds, beasts, musical instruments and gaping gargoyles all carved with great vigour. The tower at the west dated *c*.1300 is a solid affair surmounted by an octagonal spire with corner pinnacles.

The carving of the gargoyles and grotesques is by an unknown hand, but John Harvey* has identified the chief mason who worked on the chancel, which was provided at the expense of New College, Oxford, as Richard Winchcombe, who was employed here between 1408 and 1418. He was paid '3*s*. 4*d*. a week besides payments in respect of his apprentice from 1412 to 1417, ranging from 1*s*. 6*d*. to 2*s*. 9*d*. a week'. There is evidence that he visited the Taynton quarries in 1413 to 1414 to obtain stone for some of the building. The chancel was faithfully restored by J. C. Buckler in 1831–4 from an almost ruinous state, and the nave and aisles by Sir George Gilbert Scott 1866–70. Reasonable though it is, this Victorian restoration leaves the church less satisfactory within than without. The building is wide compared with its length, a plan which is not the most beguiling. The most striking features are the tall diamond-shaped clustered piers in the transepts, with carvings all presumably by the same hand as the work outside. The knight in armour with arms folded, in the south transept, is particularly effective. The main door has a fourteenth-century wrought-iron handle of excellent artistry.

Aldsworth

GLOUCESTERSHIRE
OS 163 154100
7 miles south-west of Burford

ALDSWORTH lies just off the main A433 road, and about a mile north of the narrow valley of the Leach, a stream which rises near Northleach, about four and a half miles to the north-west. It owed some of its earlier prosperity to the proximity of Bibury racecourse, and horses and gymkhana sticks still pervade the landscape. Some of the houses are none too happily restored: brown paint for windows in particular does not consort well with yellow stone, but

* *English Mediaeval Architects, a Biographical Dictionary down to 1550* (with contributions by Arthur Oswald), Alan Sutton, revised 1984.

the recent cottage extension at the east end of the row by the church is much more promising.

St Bartholomew stands on an eminence, somewhat remote. It is late Perpendicular, with an octagonal spire, and although rebuilt about 1500 it retains the narrow width of its Norman aisle to the north. Poor stained glass and heavy pews have destroyed much of its medieval atmosphere. At the east end of the north aisle is a large niche which has the emblem of the wheel on which St Catherine was martyred. On the outside there is some good carving in the spandrels of the window arches, and on the wall the arms of the abbey of Osney with whose bounty the north aisle was refashioned. A wonderful series of grotesques runs round the nave and tower on the corbel table – huge heads, one bearded with staring eyes, a griffin, a man-eating monster and other animals: a 'Rabelaisian riot', as H. J. Massingham observed, 'in a mouth-stretching guffaw'.*

The north porch has on its east wall a niche to hold candles and a narrow flue to take away the smoke, and may have served some time as a chantry chapel. There is some sturdy ironwork, which looks contemporary with the early building and therefore 800 years old, on both church and porch door, but the white paint is offensive. If the wood has to be protected, it would surely be much more suitable to use a transparent heavy-duty preservative: oak deserves far better than this nasty hard gloss, and here it should be restored to its former condition at the earliest opportunity.

The Ampneys
GLOUCESTERSHIRE
OS 163 080014
4 miles east of Cirencester

FOUR VILLAGES take their name from the Ampney Brook, a tributary of the Isis which flows to the east of Ermine Street and for a short stretch marks the old boundary between Gloucestershire and Wiltshire. The Ampneys Crucis, St Mary and St Peter are all within a mile or so of each other. Down Ampney is four miles further down the brook.

Ampney Crucis is so called from an early fifteenth-century cross depicting the Crucifixion and the Virgin on two of its faces and St Lawrence and a knight in armour on the others. It was found walled up in the rood loft at the time of the restoration of the church in 1860 and is now in the churchyard. Ampney Park, a Tudor gabled manor house with later additions, and the home of the Pleydell family from 1561 to 1724, stands to the west. The church of the Holy Rood is cruciform but with the tower at the west end. It has evidence of all architectural periods from Saxon times (although a door of that period to the north is obscured), right through to the nineteenth century. The church does not lack interest, but is a little uninviting and gloomy within. Some Pleydells are commemorated in the south transept. The Latin records the hour as well as the day of their death, monumental attention to unusual detail.

* *Cotswold Country*, Batsford, 1937.

St Mary, Ampney St Mary

The village of Ampney St Mary is a mile to the east, but has left its parish church isolated in a field with a great cedar a mile away to the south-west, even the other side of the main road. The exterior is of excellent stone with a pretty bellcote at the east end of the nave, and lovely Cotswold roofs. The south door is of elm. The setting and atmosphere of this impeccably kept church are superb. It is almost entirely twelfth- and thirteenth-century, most sympathetically restored in 1913 after it had fallen into disuse in the Victorian period. The west window with triple lights and flowing tracery is especially attractive, and so is that of the east, with its stepped lancets.

There are three items of particular interest. Over the north door is a carved lintel of odd design, perhaps symbolic of the triumph of good over evil. It shows a griffin to the left and a large lion trampling two sinister-looking snakes whose bodies form the horizontal moulding at the base of the lintel. It is a primitive work and much worn, but one of considerable power. Within there is a stone screen, a rare survivor if somewhat clumsily restored, and on the walls some extensive fragments of wall paintings executed between the twelfth and fifteenth centuries. Go on a sunny day, for with only candles to light the church, it is sometimes too dark to decipher the paintings. In the best of circumstances they are not easy to follow. On the north wall of the nave are St Christopher and St George, but the best preserved is opposite, with its subject the Commandment of the remembrance of the Sabbath that it should be kept holy. Christ is shown literally wounded by work on Sunday, with some of the instruments that are the cause of his affliction: a mallet, a wheel, and a wheelwright holding a spoke to Christ's eye.

Ampney St Peter is half a mile to the east, with cottages well preserved and beautifully restored. It is the best of the villages, but has the least rewarding church. The roof is suitably clad in stone slates with a small saddleback tower, but within it was drastically restored and enlarged by Sir George Gilbert Scott. The only interest resides in the figure on the wall north of the font. It is just under a foot high and is perhaps Saxon, symbolizing Fertility. The lower part has been damaged and the legs lost, but the head is most sensitive: a charming miniature.

Ashton Keynes

WILTSHIRE
OS 163 043944
3 miles west of Cricklade

THE INFANT THAMES runs right through the village, crossed by little stone bridges. It is a pity that the stately elms that once provided such distinction to the setting have fallen prey to that terrible disease which recently swept the country, and that the gravel pits have encroached so close, but nevertheless Ashton Keynes remains a pleasing village just south of the Gloucestershire border. The best of the houses is Ashton House, a Georgian building of five bays, and the most attractive group consists of those at Ashton Mill and Brook House on the way to the church at the north-west.

The church of Holy Cross is Norman in origin with later additions in the twelfth and thirteenth centuries. There is a plain, typically Wiltshire tower at the west end, and the building is of nicely coursed buff-coloured rubblestone, with beautiful roofs over the nave, chancel and porches. The clerestory has the unusual feature of alternately upright and diagonal quatrefoils in circles. Low clear windows elsewhere admit a fair amount of light, and even when the church is locked allow a visitor peering through a good idea of what is to be seen inside. This is not much; Butterfield restored the church in 1876–7, widening and raising the chancel arch and providing geometrics at the east end. There are four crosses in the village, presumably of some antiquity and associated with preaching; in olden days, if sermonizing was not to your taste, Ashton Keynes was clearly a village to be avoided.

[17]

Aston-sub-Edge

GLOUCESTERSHIRE
OS 151 138417
2½ miles north-west of Chipping
Campden

OF ALL THE SETTLEMENTS in the Cotswolds, Aston-sub-Edge perhaps shows most, albeit in miniature, of the pattern of English traditional building materials. As its name implies, the village lies below the Cotswold escarpment, and this explains why all is by no means stone; brick makes an appearance, and timber-frame is on show. There are many pleasant buildings in the village, but two farmhouses are specially noteworthy. Manor Farm, not far from the church, has a lovely situation, set apart in a wooded hollow, with an attractive irregularity in its stone façade; gables, mullions, transoms and dripstones, chimneys, roofs and the tall trees, all combine to make this a composition to rejoice the heart. Gardener's Farm, on the road, is more modest. The ground floor is of ashlared stone and this now obscures the jetty or overhang effect of the earlier house. The timbers above are close-set, and at one gable-end the ashlar is continued with moulds above the windows. The masonry at the chimney-stack is exceptionally fine. Exposed wood, mostly oak, is something of a stranger in the Cotswolds, but if Gardener's Farm is a stranger it is assuredly a handsome one, and the counterpoint of well-preserved wood and stone makes an admirable picture.

Bampton

OXFORDSHIRE
OS 164 313034
8 miles south-west of Witney

UNTIL THE EIGHTEENTH CENTURY Bampton was a flourishing market town. It is built mostly of stone, but lies on the extremity of the limestone; only a mile or two to the south the Oxfordshire clays begin, and across the Thames the chalk of the Berkshire Downs beckons above the Vale of White Horse. There is some chequered brick in and around the main street, and some decidedly poor fenestration in this sensitive part of the town. Most of the houses are eighteenth- and nineteenth-century, and two isolated Georgian houses, one in Bushey Row and another (if you can make it out for it is almost obfuscated with creeper) in Lavender Square, wear their ashlar and embellishments with style. For those who like a flutter there are two dovecots; one in Bushey Row rises above the middle of a barn, and another, likewise gabled, and with a wooden lantern and attendant doves, is in the garden behind a butcher's shop in Bridge Street.

Within half a mile to the west of the church there are three substantial houses. The Deanery, a gabled house which looks Elizabethan but may be a little later, is perhaps the most appealing. Weald Manor, built c.1730, is handsome enough with a Georgian parapet, but its irregularities betray a certain provincial air. Ham Court is all that remains of Bampton Castle, which until the seventeenth century was a fortified building with four towers, a moat and a gatehouse. Part of the curtain wall survives, and the gatehouse, which contains some of the medieval construction, is now a dwelling.

The Manor House, at the start of the village in Broad Street, has some Georgian refinements with a pleasant porch and fanlight

The Old Grammar School, Bampton

above the door, but the exterior is stucco; it looks well enough, yet even on the edge of limestone country this is second best. The Old Grammar School, a dignified building of the mid-seventeenth century comprising one large space below with teachers' rooms above lit by dormer windows, is now the Public Library. The Grammar School of 1871 in Church Lane, Gothic with trefoiled lancets, is now a Youth Centre.

The church of St Mary, well kept and set in a beautiful churchyard, is large and cruciform (**21**). It was punitively restored in 1867–9 by Ewan Christian who was rash enough to remove the

clerestory and, as was the fashion of his day, to scrape the interior. Beneath his restoration, the church is transitional and Early English, mostly of a date *c*.1270, with windows of the Decorated and Perpendicular periods. Within, some medieval furnishings remain: the stone reredos with tiny figures of Christ flanked by the twelve Apostles under canopies is a rare survivor, *c*.1400, and in the chancel are four misericords and two bench-ends of 100 years later. The Easter Sepulchre, roughly contemporary, is the chief treasure, with panelling under a gabled and crocketed canopy. The main attraction of this church, however, is its graceful spire, a beautiful creation of the thirteenth century. The junction of square tower and octagonal spire, always artistically a sensitive spot, is handled here as at Bloxham (q.v.) with supreme skill. With the addition of statues on pedestals – three dating from the thirteenth century, one restored in 1870 – and with each corner linked to the spire by miniature flying buttresses, it is a conceit of great originality and a delight to the eye.

Barnsley

GLOUCESTERSHIRE
OS 163 077052
5 miles north-east of Cirencester

BARNSLEY, an estate-village of singular harmony and felicity, lies on the A433, all too often to be rushed through *en route* from Cirencester to Bibury. Sharp bends in the road set the limits to east and west, service wires have been banished behind or underground, and the local stone, a yellow-grey from Quarry Hill two miles to the east, speaks in all its eloquence; only the television aerials and the whish of traffic intrude. About half the cottages date from the seventeenth century; the others are nineteenth-century and some later, but in the style of perfect neighbours – no better example of the right materials in the right place.

The church of St Mary, surrounded by a churchyard with tombstones all in the local stone, is to the east of the main road. The church dates from the twelfth century and its most notable feature is the corbel table with some entertaining grotesques. Much of the original building and subsequent workings were swept away in a none-too-imaginative restoration of the 1840s, but there is a fine baroque monument, in the floor of the aisle, made of marble with swags of fruit and flowers. It is dedicated to Elizabeth Bourchier, 1691. Of the houses in the village, Barnsley House is the best, with a front dated 1697 although Gothicized about 1840. The trees in the garden were planted about this time, although the layout dates from 1770. The garden is large and delightfully furnished, with a most seductive Gothick alcove (**22**) and Tuscan Doric temple both dating from the late eighteenth century. The garden was laid out with great skill and care by Mrs D. C. W. Verey in 1960, and is open to the public; it is a pleasure to behold all the year round.*

Barnsley Park, north of the village, can only be seen by appointment. The house was built 1720–31; the architect is unknown but

* This garden, among others, is discussed and illustrated in an excellent book, *The Englishwoman's Garden*, edited by Alvide Lees-Milne and Rosemary Verey with a foreword by Roy Strong; Chatto and Windus, London, 1980.

St Mary, Bampton
◁ Statue on flying buttress, St Mary, Bampton

Gothick alcove, Barnsley House

was possibly John Price (?–1736) 'of London' who designed a number of early Georgian churches. He worked, writes H. M. Colvin, 'in a pleasant but rather unsophisticated vernacular style derived from Wren'.* The style is mildly baroque, with references to Cannons House, in Middlesex, with which Price had been involved, and it is possible that Edward Strong, of the famous family of masons and quarry-owners at Taynton and Little Barrington, may also have shown his hand in the Cannons style (he worked on the north front). The Quarry Hill stone preserves a splendid crispness of detail, but the design is a little pretentious. The best front is at the entrance to the west, nine bays with a central projection of four giant Corinthian pilasters, all a little overblown for comfort.

The house is set in a large park whose flatness is a disadvantage,

*A Biographical Dictionary of British Architects 1600–1840, John Murray, 1978.

but there are lovely trees, and John Nash who worked here in 1806–10 provided a conservatory and a charming octagonal pepper-pot, the Bibury Lodge. The stable buildings have a cupola. Peacocks strut the grounds; vanity of vanities, but what an adornment to any landscape!

The Barringtons

GLOUCESTERSHIRE
OS 163 205135 and 209128
3 miles west of Burford

THE QUARRIES AT LITTLE BARRINGTON, only a mile or so from the Oxfordshire border, were for a long time in the ownership of the Strong family. They were an extraordinary succession of master masons who worked to the designs of Wren and Hawksmoor at a peak time of building activity, particularly in London after the Great Fire, in Oxford and in the Cotswolds. The limestone here is capable of the finest ashlar and comes from the 'inferior' oolite, a term which has nothing to do with quality (far from it) but is used to distinguish the lower beds of rocks as opposed to the 'great' which come from the higher strata. The Barrington quarry yielded a creamy-buff stone for some famous buildings: not only for St Paul's, for which Thomas Strong, considered by Wren to be the leading mason of his day, laid the foundation stone 'with his own hands' on 21 June 1675,* but many of the churches in the City of London. It was also used for the Sheldonian Theatre and the Canterbury Quad at St John's College, Oxford, and houses at

*H. M. Colvin, *A Biographical Dictionary of British Architects 1600–1840*, John Murray, 1978.

Little Barrington

Stanway, Lower Slaughter and Fairford in Gloucestershire to name but a few.

Water was close at hand; the villages lie either side of the River Windrush, and there is a wharf close by what is now the Fox Inn on the south side of the stream. Lower down is a weir to control water-levels, enabling barges to negotiate the mill-race at the beginning of a journey which would take them to the Thames at Newbridge and thence to Oxford and beyond. The quarries were worked for nearly 500 years until their closure towards the end of the last century. The river bridge was built by Thomas Strong.

At Great Barrington the parish church of St Mary, and Barrington Park, a Palladian mansion built 1736–8, attributed sometimes but without documentary evidence to William Kent, lie on the opposite side of the road from the village to the west. The house, extensively but sympathetically enlarged about 1870, is sited on a slope overlooking the Windrush. It is set in a landscaped park with a lake, a pigeon-house and a Gothick temple, and a superb pair of wrought-iron gates mark the entrance. The church was rebuilt in the 1880s. Even in medieval times it must have been quite a sizeable building, but it is notable now only for a couple of monuments: one by Christopher Cass, 1720, in marble, and another by Joseph Nollekens, 1787, a composition of some delicacy, to the memory of Mary, Countess Talbot, provider of the fortune which built the house.

Little Barrington, on the south side of the river, is grouped round a triangular green hollow which is the site of a former quarry, and through which trickles a stream. No two cottages are the same, but the stone and the scale create a unity that is most attractive (**23**). The church of St Peter is to the east, with a neighbouring farm and a substantial late eighteenth-century house, Barrington Grove. The church is worth a peep, mostly for its Norman south doorway, with its deeply cut chevron-and-lozenge ornament and a monster overhead. Its tympanum, with carved drapery, once sited over a north door, depicts Christ in Majesty supported by angels.

It is neither for the churches nor for any individual building that the Barringtons should be on a Cotswold itinerary; it is for the ensemble, and for a moment to reflect on the history of those quarries, and the masons who worked their stone.

Beverston
GLOUCESTERSHIRE
OS 173 862940
2 miles west of Tetbury

THE FLAT, QUIET AND FEATURELESS FIELDS that surround Beverston seem an unlikely place to find one of the few castles in the Cotswolds. It is not open to the public, but something of its mysterious, romantic and rather forbidding atmosphere can be savoured from the path close by. It was begun in 1225 around a courtyard, the west wall of which survives on an impressive scale with towers at each corner. The castle was enlarged about 1360 on the spoils of the battle of Poitiers and the French wars by Lord

Berkeley, in whose family it remained until 1597. He added a gatehouse and a chapel in the south-west tower, not easily accessible, but with some finely detailed carving within. The house, still with a splendid stone roof, was erected inside the courtyard in the years that followed the Berkeleys' departure; and in 1954, just beyond the sliced-off ruined gatehouse (**26**), Peter Falconer and David Verey designed Beverston House and cottage in traditional building materials, worthy companions. Two stone barns stand to the east, but a newcomer has a corrugated asbestos roof, a terrible blot on this otherwise lovely limestone group.

The church of St Mary is close by. On the south face of the tower, regrettably roughcast, is a Saxon figure of the Risen Christ with a cross-staff. It has weathered and no doubt suffered deliberate damage over the centuries, but it is a sensitive sculpture. Within, the best feature is the south arcade, *c.*1260, of three arches rising from piers decorated with stiff-leaf and scalloped capitals. The rood screen, which allegedly once did service as a trellis for a Victorian rector's climbing roses, retains some fifteenth-century work, and in the north transept, in the chantry chapel of the Berkeley family, traces of wall painting can just be seen. The church was restored by Lewis Vulliamy in 1842; he brought a fairly heavy hand to his work, but the trussed roof, resting on corbels projecting from all four walls of the nave, is a real *tour de force*. Vulliamy showed a lighter touch in the village where he designed the estate cottages, complete with bargeboards, finials and porches, neat and inoffensive.

Bibury

GLOUCESTERSHIRE
OS 163 119065
8 miles north-east of Cirencester

WILLIAM MORRIS described Bibury as the most beautiful village in England. It is certainly one of the prettiest and most popular. The main road down the hill from the hamlet of Arlington crosses an eighteenth-century stone bridge over the River Coln, alive with the sinuous shapes of trout. Across the meadow, a National Trust preserve for waterfowl, lies Arlington Row, justly one of the most photographed and celebrated groups in the Cotswolds. Arlington Row dates mostly from the seventeenth century and was perhaps converted from a former monastic barn into cottages for weavers who supplied cloth for fulling at the mill. The National Trust, which has restored and tends them with loving care, has painted the doors in a pleasant greeny-blue, which works well with the backdrop of gentle wooded slope and water-meadow. The cottages are all built of the local stone, an array of large and little gables, dormers and chimneys jostling for attention, with beautifully graded stone-slate roofs.

Much of the village clusters a little further downstream by the church, where there is a 'square', in effect a triangular green bordered by houses grouped among tall trees. To the south-east of the church is Bibury Court (**30**) with grounds that run down to the river. It is now a hotel, as secluded yet convenient a place as any

Beverston Castle, Gloucestershire

Dovecot, Bibury ▷

from which to make a Cotswold tour. The house has the date 1633 over the porch but it masks an earlier building of the Tudor period. It is a hotch-potch, with random additions and a jumble of gables and projections, but its irregularity has considerable charm.

The church of St Mary is close by. A large Saxon church had earlier stood here, and part of a Saxon cross-shaft with Scandinavian affinities is to be seen (not *in situ*) on the exterior north wall of the chancel. The tower is plain to a fault, though there are some gargoyles on the north side and a Norman door. Within, detectives of the Anglo-Saxon are in for a field-day; there is a wall to the north, a circular window to the south, and a lofty, narrow chancel arch which gives some idea of the shape of the earlier building. The arcade is vigorously carved and dates from about 1190, the period of the major rebuilding, shortly after the church had passed into the ownership of Osney Abbey.

The churchyard is among the best in the Cotswolds. There is a large expanse of grass, the setting for some splendid Georgian chest-tombs and gravestones, rich with carving. The church looks best from the south-west in afternoon sunlight, and its stone slates and yellow-grey stone from Quarry Hill, a mile or so away, are its major asset.

Just by the bridge stands Arlington Mill, recorded in Domesday (**31**). The existing building dates from the seventeenth century, was remodelled in 1859, and further cleverly restored by David

Verey, author of the Pevsner *Cotswolds* and a practising architect who contributed outstandingly to architecture and public life in Gloucestershire, of which he was a former High Sheriff. The building has been adapted as a museum with a display of working machinery from a North Cerney mill and furniture by C. R. Ashbee and others associated with the Cotswolds Arts and Crafts movement. It houses an art gallery, and attracts thousands of Bibury's many visitors each year. They come in coach-loads, but are well cared for, and the signs that direct them are discreet. For those with more leisure, Bibury, like all the showpieces of the Cotswolds, is best seen out of season, in the first leaf of spring or the glorious tints of autumn.

Bishop's Cleeve

GLOUCESTERSHIRE
OS 163 961277
4 miles north of Cheltenham

THE VILLAGE, sprawling alarmingly between the main Evesham road and the railway, lies just below the ridge (or cliff, as the name implies) which proclaims the Cotswolds proper. Stone was quarried in plenty in the hills above, and provided the remarkable group of church and rectory. St Michael and All Angels dates from about 1160. It is cruciform, and its west front has pyramidal turrets, somewhat out of perpendicular, which recall in miniature the great minster at Southwell in Nottinghamshire, built about twenty years earlier.

The south porch, with its arcaded sides and richly ornamented vault, is a dream; its doorway is a nightmare. A monster and a dragon mark the terminals of the hood-moulds; and on the outermost of the three orders, two more dragons, with coiled tails cock-a-hoop and intertwined above, are gobbling up two eagles. Some feast, some dragons! The porch has an upper chamber, decorated in 1818 by the local schoolmaster, a man called Sperry, with wall paintings depicting a battle scene with elephants. In the fourteenth century a north aisle was added and the long chancel rebuilt. The central tower replaces an earlier one which fell in 1696; it is lofty but too thin for the scale of the rest of the church. Within, the stone is a fine ashlar. There is plenty of light, and an impression of space. On each side the Norman nave has three wide arches with massive piers, and the chancel deflects or 'weeps' to the left. This has nothing to do with any symbolism associated with the incline of Christ's head upon the cross, a specially tempting interpretation in a cruciform church, but is merely evidence of difficulties of alignment faced by the medieval masons. There is an elaborate wooden gallery, presumably Jacobean and intended for musicians, at the west end – always the best place for accompaniment to the services. Two monuments are of note: in the south chapel, no expense was spared in commemorating Richard de la Bere who died in 1636. The effigy is in alabaster and rather ordinary, although it is surrounded by handsomely gilded wrought-iron railings. The monument to Edmund Bedingfield, sixty years later, is baroque, and a much jollier affair. There are also some vestigial wall paintings – the remains of a Crucifixion in the north transept, and a St Christopher in the north aisle.

The former rectory, close by, is a magnificent Charles II house with a hipped roof covered with stone slates. There are Venetian windows at either end. This splendid rebuilding of 1667 masks a much earlier house, in the ownership of the bishops of Worcester, which goes back to the middle of the thirteenth century. This must make it the oldest parsonage in the county, and its double dovecot and later refurbishments made it a house well suited to the dignity and standing of the incumbent. Needless and sad to say, times and the parson have moved on.

A tithe barn, much truncated, and only about a half of its original size, now serves as the village hall. The early fifteenth-century roof timbers are both oak and chestnut, recourse to which was sometimes necessary when oak became scarce. Chestnut must have been plentiful locally, and while it is not so durable, it does not attract beetle. What you gain on the wind-braces you lose on the collar-beams.

Bisley-with-Lypiatt
GLOUCESTERSHIRE
OS 163 904059
4 miles east of Stroud

THE PARISH IS LARGE. It spreads over high ground above the River Frome and, irritatingly, between two Ordnance Survey sheets, 163 and 162, with no overlap. It is full of substantial houses built for wealthy clothiers, and is well worth a drive, or better still a day's walk, through the lanes, David Verey's *Buildings of England** in hand, to see how many can be seen. Over Court and Jaynes Court are close to Bisley's church. Roughly within a two-mile radius lie Ferris Court at Eastcombe, with a splendid barn, then Avenis Farm and Solomon's Court at Bourne's Green; next, Waterlane House and Watercombe House, both houses designed in the early nineteenth century by an amateur architect, Thomas Baker, with identical wrought-iron porches; then on up to Througham Slad, very private, ex-directory and medieval in origin. Lower and Upper Througham are both gabled and mullioned. Lower Througham, with a dovecot in each gable, is specially worth seeing. Sydenhams comes next, again medieval but with alterations by Norman Jewson who also worked at the Throughams. The Lypiatts are best saved for last; Lypiatt Park (remodelled by Wyatville) has a fourteenth-century chapel and granary, Middle Lypiatt is Tudor with gables and projecting wings, and finally, the queen of them all, Nether Lypiatt Manor (**32**).

Nether Lypiatt is one of England's most enchanting smaller country houses. The ashlar masonry has weathered to a richly satisfying grey, and the house has a perfect roof of Cotswold stone slate. The house was built between 1702 and 1705 although the rainwater heads proclaim 1717. It is an exact square, forty-six feet in each direction. There are five bays to each of the fronts, and the symmetry was further emphasized by five chimney-stacks evenly

* *Gloucestershire: The Cotswolds*, second edition, Penguin Books, 1979.

[29]

Bibury Court, Gloucestershire
Arlington Mill, Bibury ▷
Bibury ▷

dispersed, one at each corner, and a large central stack which provided a focal point as might a lantern on a larger house. One stack to the north has recently been lost. Nether Lypiatt Manor is modest in size. It has a semi-basement, a ground floor entered by a porch at the top of a flight of thirteen steps, and the bedrooms above. In the roof an attic storey with dormers, two to each side, was added as recently as 1923 by P. R. Morley Horder, but the leaded casements are not ideal in a house of this quality.

The windows elsewhere are by no means uniform. The basement has mostly small mullions and transoms and while on the entrance front and at the back the windows are sashed, the glazing bars reveal at least three different thicknesses, evidence as they became thinner of progressively later dates. The panes are a little too square, reminiscent of colonial Williamsburg in Virginia. The plan of the house is unusual. The staircase is to the north, and there are only three rooms on the *piano nobile*, the largest of which, at the back, overlooks the garden and fills that entire side of the house. There was originally space for only four bedrooms.

At the front of the house is a screen of stone piers, with wrought-iron gates ascribed to Warren, one of the family of smiths who produced such wonders at Cambridge. The temptation to plant too many flowers, however attractive, beneath the façade must be strong, but well-tended lawns are surely more appropriate. This is the grand house in miniature, perhaps a little too

Nether Lypiatt Manor,
Bisley-with-Lypiatt

tall for its width, but a building that gives unending pleasure.

The parish church of All Saints was restored by the Revd W. H. Lowder in 1862. He was curate here to Thomas Keble, uncle of the eminent divine. Double piscinas survive, one in the chancel with Decorated tracery of *c.*1300, and another at the south doorway. In the churchyard, which must have been a sobering prospect for the onlookers from the gazebo of Over Court, is a rare poor souls' light, an interesting survivor of the thirteenth century with trefoiled recesses. Here candles were offered for those too poor to provide their own. Just below, down steps at the south-west of the churchyard, are the seven springs, a bubbling water supply celebrated in 1863 Gothick; well-dressing by the village children is one of the annual early summer events.

The village still tells the tale of the Bisley Boy, or rather the Bisley Girl, the skeleton of a tall girl found in the churchyard when the school was being built in 1854, and purportedly that of Queen Elizabeth I. She is said to have died, so the tale goes, while staying at Over Court in 1543, and her guardians, scared out of their wits at the result of their carelessness, substituted a boy 'of the same age and appearance' in her place. The story, so Mrs Rudd reveals in her *Historical Records of Bisley-with-Lypiatt* published in the 1940s, was an invention of the vicar, Mr Keble, prompted by the resemblance to the queen of a family in the parish, who conveniently claimed

Limestone slab fencing,
Bledington

descent from an illegitimate branch of Henry VIII. The twinkle in
the vicar's eye has brought many visitors to the village on this score
alone, but Bisley has a far better claim to our attention as a
delightful village of cottages, stone roofs and country gardens.

The school was designed by G. F. Bodley, whose first complete
church is at France Lynch three miles to the south. There are some
inviting old inns, including the Bear Inn which was formerly the
court-house for 200 years until 1766. The Old Bell Inn, of the late
seventeenth century, was restored in 1953 for the British Legion
who, while dispensing their admirable philanthropy, certainly
know how to enjoy a convivial country pint. Their tenure of the
Old Bell Inn seems happily appropriate.

Bledington

GLOUCESTERSHIRE
OS 163 245226
5 miles south-east of
Stow-on-the-Wold

BLEDINGTON GROUPS AROUND A LARGE GREEN, just above
the River Evenlode, whose tributary stream flows through the
village among stone barns, cottages and farmhouses. Limestone
slab fencing appears near the church. There are some brick buildings too, for there was once a brickworks nearby. The church of St
Leonard, best seen from the south-east, is set above the surrounding houses on a dais of green. It looks more like an Oxfordshire
than a Gloucestershire church, but then the county boundary is
only half a mile away. The tower is austere, and even slightly gaunt,
and a Norman bellcote perches on the east gable of the nave. Only

St Leonard, Bledington

Bloxham

OXFORDSHIRE
OS 151 430357
3½ miles south-west of Banbury

---

the rich tracery of the late Perpendicular windows gives the church some degree of external sumptuousness. An old oak door on the south, with original hinges, gives admittance to a remarkable interior.

The plan is most curious. There is a south aisle but not one to the north, although the north wall has a clerestory with windows of a distinctly domestic appearance and original glass of the fifteenth century. The church is in origin Norman, and the tower was built within the west bay of the nave. The chancel is divided from the nave by a low, narrow arch, admitting to a rather private inner sanctum, and between the chancel and the south aisle, separated by an ornate foliated arch, is a tiny and mysterious chapel, thought to be, though with no documentary evidence, a chantry chapel. The window at the east end of the aisle, and others elsewhere in the nave, has image brackets with nodding ogee-headed canopies. The fifteenth-century glass is thought to be by John Prudde who worked in the Beauchamp Chapel at St Mary, Warwick. A substantial amount survives, fragmentary and rather pallid, but providing a lot of light. The walls could do with a fresh limewash, but the old oak roofs are satisfyingly simple and robust, and the masoncraft is of the highest quality.

BLOXHAM WAS ONCE a large agricultural village, but the boom of the last decade and its proximity to Banbury put it in danger of becoming a commuters' dormitory. The main road from the south once made a wide zigzag detour to the west, but about 1800 it was realigned on a straighter course and is now something of a race-track with speeding traffic. The medieval plan of narrow winding streets, however, survives. Dwellings, built of the local tawny ironstone, some with thatch, huddle within the confines of the old village. A whole row of seventeenth-century cottages at Little Green retains its thatch; Merrivales Lane and Unicorn Street are just two of many streets that preserve a medieval feeling.

The church of St Mary is splendidly sited. It is dramatically in view on the approach from the north as the road descends to cross the stream, fringed with alder and willow, and then climbs the other side to where the church stands on the brow of the hill. The tower and spire, built in the first half of the fourteenth century, are of admirable proportions, and the link between the base of the spire and the top of the tower is particularly accomplished. At its fifth stage the tower becomes an octagon, the corners being marked by pinnacles which extend from the fourth stage, and the spire then almost literally takes off, soaring away magnificently to a height of 198 feet. It is uplifting in every sense of the word.

This steeple is much taller than Adderbury's, although otherwise the two churches have many similarities. At Bloxham, as at Adderbury, there is much tracery and a lively parade of sculpture. The frieze below the parapet to the north shows fantastic beasts, men fighting, and a pig with its litter. The gargoyles, equally effective, and which must be from the same school of sculptors, are to the south at Bloxham and also high up on the tower. The west window has carved figures as well as tracery, and at the top a wheel, the hub of which has a representation of Christ. At the west door is a Last Judgement, a fairly minor affair compared with other Cotswold tympana. Christ sits enthroned between angels, flanked either side by familiar scenes of the resurrection of the blessed and the consignment of the damned to the jaws of hell.

Within, the walls have been scraped. The plan is wide in relation to its length, and the proportions are not improved by the addition to the south of the south aisle of the large Milcombe Chapel of *c.*1420–30. The nave is almost square, which is not a happy arrangement, but there are many carved heads, a screen, a Perpendicular font, and more tracery. The most impressive features are the tall diamond-shaped clustered piers, with vigorous carving at the capitals, though at Bloxham this is confined to the north transept: heads and shield-bearing arms which are stylistically similar to the armoured knights at Adderbury. Both churches are better outside than in. G. E. Street, whose work is all too apparent in the diocese of Oxford, was responsible for a fairly hefty restoration here in 1864–6; previously he had enlarged the vicarage, now The Chantry, opposite. The pulpit, the reredos and the choir stalls, the vestry and east window, are his creation. Devotees of the Pre-Raphaelites will linger lovingly before the stained glass of William Morris, Edward Burne-Jones and Philip Webb. It is a little garish and not to everyone's taste, but makes Kempe's later offerings look woefully inadequate.

Street was also commissioned for All Saints' School which dominates the north end of the village. His original scheme had to be abandoned but the dining-hall and chapel were built to his design. There have been piecemeal additions during this century which incline more to function, perhaps, than did the high-minded creations of their Gothic forerunner. Elsewhere in the village a number of old houses have been remodelled over the centuries; Manor Farm House in Chapel Street has a door, not perhaps *in situ*, but at least 600 years old, and the Court House has a doorway and blocked windows from the same period.

Bloxham repays a leisurely perambulation with St Mary's, one of the finest churches in the county, as its focal point.

Bourton-on-the-Water

GLOUCESTERSHIRE
OS 163 167209
3 miles south-west of
Stow-on-the-Wold

CHOOSE YOUR TIME CAREFULLY to see Bourton-on-the-Water, for the crowds in high summer are in danger of destroying the delights that bring them here. Go, too, by way of the Rissingtons, for the approach from Stow-on-the-Wold through modern housing is anything but beautiful, although it affords an opportunity to see Bourton Bridge, a late-medieval bridge rebuilt in 1806 and widened in 1959, at the turn-off from the Fosse Way (A429).

The setting is of infinite charm; a wide green through which runs the River Windrush, wide, clear water sparkling in the sun, crossed by five low foot-bridges, and flanked by generous grass verges. Two bridges, Payne's Foot-bridge and the rusticated Narrow Bridge, 1756, deserve special attention, and the stone road-bridge at the end of Sherborne Street is also good. Many visitors seldom stray from the green where most of the cafés and gift shops and other tourist attractions are on offer – Birdland, a collection of exotic birds and flowers, a butterfly museum, a small zoo, an aquarium, a trout farm, a pottery, a working mill, a model railway, and best of all a model village, an exact replica to one-ninth scale, done in the local stone.

The church, dedicated to St Lawrence, is disappointing. It is Georgian, designed by William Marshall who lived in the village, and his church replaced a Norman church demolished in 1784. Marshall retained the chancel, which had been rebuilt in the early fourteenth century, but his main contribution is the tower. It is rusticated at the base, with giant Ionic pilasters, cornices and balustrades, but it is uninspired and capped by a lead domelet, an oddity of little distinction. The church was again rebuilt 1875–90 by Sir Thomas Jackson, a man sensitive to traditional building materials, and the architect of the Examination Schools in Oxford. He kept the tower and chancel but provided a new nave and a north aisle.

The interior of the church is Victorian and exceedingly so. It is dark, for the abundance of Victorian windows, mostly by Kempe and Tower, admits no light, making the bold kingpost roof of the nave, 1891, difficult to see, let alone admire. Jackson's arcade for the north aisle, five bays with round piers and Gothic arches, is rather feeble, but the chancel roof, nine-sided, was colourfully if a little over-enthusiastically painted in 1928 by F. E. Howard, with armorial bearings of lords of the manor and patrons, St Lawrence the patron saint, and flowers, speedwell and roses. Howard also carved and painted the reredos, oak screens and rood.

Architecturally Bourton may not be top-rank in the Cotswolds, but there is much to enjoy. The stone is the greatest attraction, a warm grey-brown in colour, and much of the restoration and renovation over recent years is excellent. The Old Rectory, Hartly House and Ivy Nook are well worth seeking, but best is Harrington House (37), by a long way the most handsome building in the village. The ashlar is of the highest quality. The Palladian façade, of about 1740, has a sizeable pediment, complete with *œil de bœuf*, carried on pilasters over three of the five bays. The parapet has a balustrade and vase finials and a stone roof crowned by a domed lantern. Keystones, architraves and glazing bars are in place; this is a house all present and correct.

The doorway has its pediment too, supported by rusticated Ionic pilasters, and there is an elaborate fanlight. The ensemble is marred

Harrington House,
Bourton-on-the-Water

only by the upper half of the door, which is glazed, presumably to allow more light. A glimpse through the door reveals some delightful rococo plasterwork in the hall and the staircase beyond, both about 1740.

Broadway
WORCESTERSHIRE
OS 150 095374
6 miles west of Chipping Campden

BROADWAY, SAID NIKOLAUS PEVSNER,* is the 'show village of England'. It has been persistently reproved for its self-consciousness, but Broadway is beautiful, and its special appeal lies in its variety of design and style within the uniformity of its yellow limestone. The village is one long straight street, of generous grass-fringed breadth. It gradually ascends, but more steeply and tortuously towards the Cotswold ridge at Fish Hill which closes the view to the east about a mile away. At the top, if you can resist the Fish Inn and its stunning gazebo (hemmed in too much by modern accretions), take Buckle Street, a lane which leads south about a mile to Broadway Tower, 1,000 feet above sea-level, and 600 above the village. It was built as a folly by Lady Coventry in 1797 with three turrets placed on three sides of what might have been a hexagon. It is Gothick with 'Norman' details and has battlements and balconies, whence spectacular views across to

* *The Buildings of England: Worcestershire*, Penguin Books, 1968.

Bredon and the Malverns beyond. On a clear day you can see no fewer than thirteen counties, so they say.

Crowds flock to Broadway, and when they gather, the pleasure of an architectural perambulation undoubtedly diminishes. Go on a sunny mid-week morning in early spring, without a visitor in sight, and the snowdrops in bloom. Let us return down the hill. Tudor, Stuart, Georgian are the order of the day. The architecture of our own century, albeit in traditional style, also makes its mark, together with less desirable addenda of the 'quaint' and 'picturesque', carriage lamps, spindly wrought iron, ingle-nooks and peep-holes, studs on olde-worlde varnished doors. It is easy, but unwise, to sneer, for this is a village where the pleasure of the ensemble lingers far longer than the impact of any individual building.

On the left is the Jacobean Court Farm, long and low, showing some timber-frame around the corner, and enlarged at the beginning of this century. To the north is a row of cottages, ashlared and with stone-tiled dormers, done up, of course, but robust and welcome. To the south comes the parapet of Leeds House and another early Georgian house, both handsome with good doorways. The former police house opposite, now renamed Peel House and Cottage, is modest and stone-tiled. It was built in 1911 and suits the locality well.

Further down, Prior's Manse peeps out from under heavy foliage. It is determinedly medieval, L-shaped with an early fourteenth-century doorway, and a medieval hall within. Opposite, a large Antiques Emporium occupies Tudor House, surprisingly named for its date of 1660. It is gabled above a grand façade of three storeys and a projecting centre bay. Our zigzag now returns south to Broad Close, a symmetrical Regency house with deliciously elliptical bow windows. Picton House is Georgian, long and low, with thick glazing bars, dignified, but a little plain.

On then to the Lygon Arms (pronounced Liggon), high and handsome with pointed gables and the most famous among a number of excellent inns and hotels in the village. It was formerly a manor house, and is the best Cotswold house in Broadway, full of character and full of comforts. The doorway (**39**) has tapering pilasters, and at the lintel, decorated work of interlaced bands suggesting an earlier date than 1620 which it confidently proclaims. Within there is a chimney-piece of the seventeenth century and another from the reign of Henry VIII, and a new and large dining-room was added in 1910 by C. E. Bateman who worked with much sensitivity elsewhere in and around the village. On the opposite side, lower down, is Broadway Hotel, the only major building to show black and white and, on the green, the Jacobean Farnham House and its pretty Georgian neighbour look back up the hill. On the way to the Cheltenham junction is Russell House, the home of Gordon Russell, the founder of a thriving family

business, who began by making furniture for the Lygon Arms. A charming Gothick pavilion faces the road.

Church Street leads to the south, and on the right is Abbot's Grange, secluded and shy behind a grey wall and yew. It is Broadway's most interesting house, an L-shaped fourteenth-century building in origin with hall, solar and chapel, much altered in the Elizabethan period and with west wings sympathetically added in this century. Around the church of St Michael, built in 1839 conveniently close to the village, the more so to encourage the faithful, there are other agreeable houses, notably the early Georgian Austin House, approached through gate-piers and up semicircular steps.

The parish church proper lies nearly a mile further to the south at Bury End which seems most likely to have been the original settlement. It is dedicated to the granddaughter of King Alfred, St Eadburga, a child saint (to paraphrase James Lee-Milne†) much given to washing other people's socks. The building is part-ashlar, part-rubblestone and roofed with stone slates, all in a glorious golden brown. Within it has a poignant sense of solitude and timelessness. In the south transept is a monument to William Taylor, who died in 1741; it is undeniably a handsome object but, made of white and grey marble, something of an intruder. The altar rails are Jacobean with knobs on, but the pulpit, an elaborate Elizabethan affair, has been removed to the church of St Michael. It should surely be returned. The church is as beautiful without as within, set amongst trees and fields, and surrounded by a romantic churchyard of tumbledown grey tombstones, yew and holly, where even the grass is allowed to grow.

Broughton
OXFORDSHIRE
OS 151 419383
2½ miles south-west of Banbury

BROUGHTON, pronounced bror-t'n, is on a secondary road which runs west to Chipping Campden, but the colour of its stone is markedly different. The village is only seven miles to the south of Hornton, the most famous of all the marlstone quarries, no longer worked, although a similar stone is still available at Edge Hill just over the Warwickshire border. Hornton is a limestone rich in iron and of subtle colour, a delicate mixture of grey, gold and green, and it provides much of the pleasure in the buildings of the surrounding countryside.

The church of St Mary, its rectory and the large house, Broughton Castle, the loveliest and most complete medieval house in Oxfordshire, make a splendid group. The church and its broach spire are almost entirely *c.*1300, although the best of the tracery at either end of the south aisle, and the pretty stone screen inside with its crocketed ogee, are of the later Decorated period. The interior is over-restored but there are some interesting monuments: a recumbent knight, his pillow supported by angels and a lion at his feet, lies within an ornate arched recess, work of the early fourteenth

† *Worcestershire*: a Shell Guide.

Broughton Castle

century, and in the chancel are the excellent effigies of a knight and a lady in alabaster dating from about 100 years later.

The Rectory, dated 1694, is to the east; it has had alterations over the years, notably by Richard Pace and S. P. Cockerell, both of whom did substantial work locally and were engaged here in the early part of the nineteenth century. In the village are some attractive cottages of 1841 in the Tudor style, and some rather untraditional almshouses, Victorian Gothic, linked by a low wall.

A moat provides a spectacular setting for the castle, approached across a bridge and guarded by a gatehouse. The house was built as a fortified manor and has been lived in by the Fiennes family for over 500 years. The manuscript of the journal of their celebrated seventeenth-century ancestor, Celia, the intrepid horsewoman and diarist who rode the length and breadth of England, is kept in the house, and a family atmosphere prevails.

The oldest part of the house is to the east. It was built in 1306 to house a first-floor living-room or 'solar' (a word derivative of the Latin *sol*, sun, for the enjoyment of which the room was presumably intended). This followed the normal domestic plan of that date; there was a chapel below supported by a vaulted undercroft.

Further east a new kitchen was added at the end of the sixteenth century. About that time the main north front was reconstructed, more or less symmetrically, with the main entrance discreetly tucked away on the side of the central projection. The windows are rather a jumble: some have diamond, some rectangular panes; a few are Gothick and sashed. It would, however, be churlish and dull of spirit to find one single fault in the ensemble.

The Elizabethan Great Hall incorporates the original medieval house of 1300 with a plaster ceiling and pendants added in the 1760s. The dining-room, *c.*1500 and part of the undercroft, has a ribbed vault and linenfold panelling, wood carved to resemble folds in a carefully arranged fabric. This room is dark enough already, and unfortunately faces north. A visit proceeds by way of the parlour, with elaborate plaster ceiling, through the bedrooms, the main one of which has a peep-hole to the chapel which must obviate the inconvenience of having to get up for early church, to the Long Gallery. This is giggling Gothick, striding gleefully away the length of the house. The Oak Room is best and saved for last; it is breathtakingly spacious and light, with the wood a delicious silver colour, and it includes an extraordinary interior porch and cartouche.

Outside, the roof is smothered with Stonesfield slates, carefully graded from bottom to top, and a gently mottled lichen clings to the walls.

Buckland
GLOUCESTERSHIRE
OS 150 083360
2 miles south-west of Broadway

THE VILLAGE LIES SECLUDED under the Cotswold ridge, 'feudal' and rather exclusive (**43**), though a modern development of holiday cottages, still a little raw but a model of its kind, tempts the self-catering tourist. Until recently the Rectory, essentially a fifteenth-century stone house of ample proportions, was lived in by the rector, which in its historic continuity must have made it the most complete and oldest house of its kind in the country. The entrance and oriel above are original but the most striking feature is the Great Hall, once regularly on show, with a magnificent open roof over thirty feet high at the ridge and a central hammerbeam carved at each end with angels holding shields. There are a number of interesting panels of stained glass dating from the fifteenth century. It is to be hoped that this remarkable house will, on occasion, continue to be made accessible to visitors.

The church of St Michael, rather plain outside, has much interest within. The walls were stripped of plaster and medieval frescoes were lost in the restoration of 1885, but substantially the fifteenth century lives on, with tiles in the south aisle, well copied elsewhere in the church, an ornate font, and some original oak benches, dignified and sturdily carved. The west gallery dates from *c.*1640, as does the oak seating in the aisles and chancel, with hat-pegs projecting horizontally from the wainscoting under the testers – a rare, if not unique, survival.

Buckland

A sizeable quantity of glass appears in three panels of the upper lights of the east window, the gift of William Grafton, rector 1466–83. They represent the sacraments of Baptism, with the child looking customarily uncomfortable, Confirmation, Marriage, and Extreme Unction. They were restored, at his own expense, by William Morris.

In the north aisle are carved stones, said to have come from Hailes Abbey after the Dissolution, with trefoil heads and painted angels in the recesses. A cope or altar frontal of faded blue embroidery, shaded from the light, is on show near the door. The recurring decorative motif could be pomegranate seeds, emblem of Catherine of Aragon who married Henry VIII in 1502; below is a Crucifixion, and above are the letters W H Y and a church – perhaps the rebus of William Whychurch, abbot of Hailes 1464–79. Finally, to fill your cup, is a mazer bowl, a goblet of maple wood, painted green outside and white within. It is kept under glass in the south aisle. This cup dates from the sixteenth century and has a silver-gilt impression of St Michael (the patron) slaying his dragon or St Margaret bursting out of hers. It was used reputedly as a loving-cup at village weddings, not such a pop or a price as champagne, but a no less appropriate send-off to a happy pair.

Burford

OXFORDSHIRE
OS 163 253125
7 miles west of Witney

FOR THE TRAVELLER from the home counties who considers that the universe revolves if not round London then at least around Oxford, Burford has been called the 'Gateway to the Cotswolds'. This is architecturally somewhat misleading, for while so many of the Cotswold villages and towns portray a unity of stone and style, Burford is more a miscellany. Approached from the west it is more the Cotswolds' final fling; over the crest is the upper Thames and the chalk of the Vale of White Horse beyond.

Burford is not only one of the most famous of the small medieval wool towns; it is also one of the oldest. There were merchants' guilds here within thirty years of the Conquest; it became one of the most flourishing markets of the Cotswolds, and the cloth magnates of the sixteenth century, Simon Wisdom, a great benefactor, and Edmund Sylvester, left an indelible mark on the town. When the wool trade declined, the coaches brought the inns, a considerable number of which survive. Witney Street was once the main Oxford and London road, and Sheep Street the route to Wales and the West. When the London Road was improved in 1812, however, it was diverted to the south at the top of the ridge, and the railway forty years later followed the Evenlode valley five miles to the north.

The setting is unforgettable. The High Street descends steeply from the ridge, admittedly too full of traffic and parked cars, and disfigured by yellow lines and, periodically, severely butchered trees. At the bottom, against a backdrop of green fields and gently wooded slopes to the north, it broadens and crosses the Windrush by a bridge, much repaired over 600 years. Here willows and reeds, stone and water, make as fitting a boundary as any town could wish to have.

In the High Street, there is any amount of variety; shops and offices that once were medieval inns, Georgian façades to earlier buildings behind, and more exposed timber-framing than anywhere else in the Cotswolds, with a diversity of render and infill, sometimes plaster, sometimes roughcast, sometimes rubblestone and ashlar. Brick makes a solo appearance at the Bull Hotel. At the corner of Sheep Street is the Tolsey, pillared at the front, where once market tolls were collected and town business conducted. It is now a museum. Almost every house in this town merits consideration.

The upper part of High Street is largely residential, with shops beginning lower down. The House of Simon was built by Simon Wisdom whose initials, and the date 1582 (?2), appear above the doorway. He lived in what is now Roger Warner's Antiques Emporium, a courtyard house refronted about 1720, and his initials again can be seen on panelling within, dated 1555. He is further commemorated, when the creeper is not in full leaf and the plaque peers through, at the cottages he built by the bridge. Edmund Sylvester also did himself proud; he built Falkland House

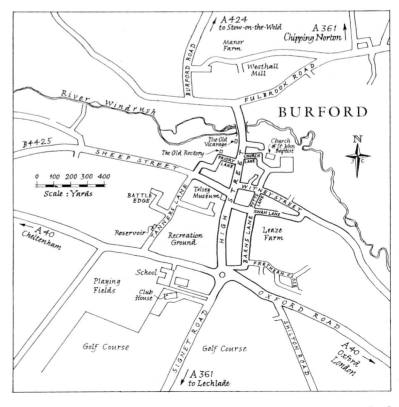

High Street,
Burford

in 1558, all stone, prominently sited at the corner of Priory Lane. A number of the more 'gracious' houses are now gift or antique shops whose owners, generally speaking, make excellent guardians of an historic house in an historic town, but it always comes as a special pleasure to see an ancient building, relatively unscathed, continuing to do a more day-to-day job. W. J. Castle, family butchers, and Josephine Sumner are a case in point, sharing two bays of a fifteenth-century three-gabled house with delicately carved bargeboards, unusual if not unique in the whole Cotswold region. Inside Castle's, not on public view, are some wall paintings, an unfamiliar domestic feature, and at the petrol-station-cum-bicycle-shop close by, painted ceiling beams have recently been revealed, one

The Old Rectory,
Burford

of which was removed and can be seen in 'The Welsh Shop' opposite.

Down the hill close by the bridge stands the Old Vicarage, of ashlar rusticated at the quoins; its main feature is three Dutch gables, two with pediments and one a segmental arch, which are purely decorative and display blank medallions in place of dormer windows. The date is 1672, and the first floor is obviously quite grand with its three long mullion-and-transomed windows. It may not be an elegant building but it has personality. Such is the pace of ecclesiastical change in Burford that in Priory Street there is also

The Old Vicarage,
Burford

an Old Rectory (**46**), ascribed to Christopher Kempster, one of Christopher Wren's most distinguished City masons. In origin this house is about thirty years later than the Vicarage, and its pure and classical façade, devoid of restless detail, makes it one of the most successful houses of its size and date in the whole of Oxfordshire.

Kempster was born in Burford and had his own house at Kit's Quarries, just outside the town along Sheep Street, and he is buried under an inscribed stone, dated 1715, in the south transept of the parish church. His name was for a long time also associated with the Wesleyan chapel in the High Street (**49**). This is really a town house, and a fine one at that, which only became a chapel in 1849 when the parapet was relieved of its decorative urns in accord with its newly acquired sobriety. It looks too ornate for Kempster, witness his reticence at the Old Rectory, but despite its somewhat busy adornments, it has dignity. The giant pilasters crowned with Corinthian capitals are particularly effective and the masoncraft is bold and crisp.

The architect is unknown, but the most likely ascription is to Francis Smith, 'Smith of Warwick', as he is generally known, and the weight and authority that he brings to this comparatively small building by rusticating the stonework horizontally throughout and making a feature of the keystones above the windows is reminiscent of his Court House in his home town. Francis Smith was twice mayor of Warwick in 1713 and 1728 and is a good example of a not uncommon phenomenon in the eighteenth century: a man of humble origins, son of a bricklayer, who started life as a stone-mason and gradually rose in the world. He became a master-builder, and an architect in all but name, with a sizeable practice in the Midlands and work to his credit — no idle phrase, that — at Ditchley, Heythrop, Stoneleigh, Chicheley Hall and Sutton Scars-dale, now a ruin.

Simon Wisdom gave the town its Grammar School. It was founded in 1571 on a site just south-west of the parish church and the building, enlarged and partly rebuilt in the nineteenth century, is still used as a boarding-house of the school. In Church Lane, opposite, are the Great Almshouses, founded in 1457 by Warwick the Kingmaker and rebuilt in 1828. The Church Schools, a Victorian essay in the Tudor style, consort well.

The church of St John the Baptist, a fine but historically compli-cated building, dates largely from the twelfth and fifteenth centur-ies; it lacks shape, but is a microcosm of parish-church history. Externally the chief features are four. First the tower, centrally placed; the lower part is Norman, with much beautiful carving. The upper part, Decorated with ogee-headed windows below a parapet, is also attractive, although the stair turret looks somewhat awkward against the west wall, and overlaps both the south aisle and the tower's west arch. The south porch dates from 1450. It is no longer free-standing and seems lost in the attendant jumble, but

Wesleyan Chapel, High Street, Burford

it is richly ornamental. It has a room over a fan-vaulted entrance, and the frieze has special charm with its little angels, crocketed pinnacles and shields.

The chapel of St Mary and St Anne, sometimes referred to as the Sylvester aisle, on account of its six almost identical family tombs, was once free-standing in the churchyard. It was originally built in about 1200 by the Guild of Merchants, but its incorporation in the fifteenth century into the body of the church leaves it an uneasy composition in relation to the rest of the building. The west door is Norman, again with much decoration, if somewhat restored. The single most positive asset, and one which gives this somewhat odd-shaped church its unity, is the magnificent stone in its shades of brown, grey and fawn.

Within there is a nice old muddle. Under the tower, the architecture is pure Norman, and the arches inconveniently low; the rest is Gothic, mainly Perpendicular, and the tie-beam roof is particularly good. The upper part of the west window, in the tiers of the tracery lights and the heads of the main lights, has some jewel-like fifteenth-century glass, in marked contrast to Kempe's drab greenery in the lower main part of the window, which has no sparkle at all. The monument to Lord Chief Justice Tanfield and family, 1628, is impossible to miss; it is prominently sited in a chapel to the north, with a canopy and coffered vault, surmounted by obelisks and the Virtues. The materials, suitable perhaps for a grandee (chief baron of the Exchequer) but not for a Cotswold church, are alabaster and imported black marble. Tanfield, by reputation corrupt and avaricious, was no friend of the town. He bought the lordship of the manor and successfully took the burgesses to court for usurping his rights. His tomb was erected by his widow without the permission of the churchwardens. There is a lot of colour; high in effect, but low in quality.

The Perpendicular font is a treasure, and must be among the prettiest in the county. It is circular and tub-form, and has, at the south-south-west, a delicious smiling figure of St Catherine, and next to her St Andrew, with his arms aloft, also smiling. The patron saint, St John the Baptist, is there with his lamb, but Christ crucified, in a composition on the east side with Mary and John, is sadly defaced.

This is a spacious interior. In the 1870s it had the misfortune to be restored by the architect G. E. Street. No major structural alterations were contemplated, but medieval plaster was stripped from the walls of the nave, leaving an ugly rubblestone in evidence. This, among other over-zealous attempts at 'improvements' such as at Tewkesbury, provoked 'anti-scrape' and William Morris's famous letter in 1877 which led to the founding of the Society for the Protection of Ancient Buildings. The reply of the vicar, the Revd W. A. Cass, when confronted with Morris's protests, was: 'The church, Sir, is mine, and if I choose to I shall stand on my head in it.'* Nowadays a parson's freehold certainly does not, if ever it did, extend to his church, and matters of architectural and artistic concern are properly subject to the restraints and deliberations of diocesan advisory committees. Lovers of English parish churches should be grateful to those voluntary bodies, and indeed to William Morris and his Society, still going strong, for their unremitting vigilance.

Font, St John the Baptist, Burford

Burton Dassett
WARWICKSHIRE
OS 151 398515
9 miles north-west of Banbury

THE CHURCH OF ALL SAINTS has only its former vicarage and two farms for company. In the thirteenth century this village was a thriving community with a market, but those who survived the years of plague were later driven off by enclosing landlords. The hamlet of Northend snuggles under the hill a mile to the north, overlooked by a beacon tower, originally perhaps a medieval mill and then a look-out, and now a focus of weekend afternoon jaunts to the surrounding country park with dogs, kites and ponies. The church (**51**) stands all alone on the lower slopes of Church Hill in a large churchyard with some swagger tombstones, a setting of harmony and solemnity.

Burford Past and Present, M. S. Gretton, from information provided by May Morris and quoted by Jennifer Sherwood, *The Buildings of England: Oxfordshire*, Penguin Books, 1974.

All Saints, Burton Dassett

A quarry yielding the iron-tinted Hornton limestone, or something extremely close to it, was within the parish and provided the warm, golden-brown stone for the church, vicarage and other buildings nearby. The former vicarage, surrounded by tall trees, is dated 1696, but it now has top-heavy bargeboards, and a tiled roof which is welcome neither in texture nor colour. The church wears an air of antique solidity. It is entered by a door of venerable oak whereon a notice advises that dogs house-trained and under proper control may be admitted. The immediate impression within is one of 'unrestoration', the light and sensitive work of J. Cossins who was engaged here in 1890, and clearly did his job with skill. Light

Cartouche wall painting, All Saints,
Burton Dassett

Carved abacus, All Saints, ◁
Burton Dassett

pours in through a rustic-looking clerestory, and plain but beautiful roofs extend over a nave of five bays and two wide aisles.

The church accommodates the slope: the nave is on a gentle
decline from east to west (**51**). There are twelve steps between altar
and nave and five more at the entrance to the west. The nave is
Norman, but substantially the rest of the church is *c.*1300, and on
the octagonal piers of the north arcade is some entertaining
carving: a dragon, a rabbit and dogs all scurry round the capitals,
hell-bent for each other's tails. A local, bearing sheaves, presides
above. There are also a number of contemporary medieval tiles,
best preserved near the font and in the aisle.

In 1966 a series of wall paintings was uncovered. Restoration
was carried out by Mrs Eve Baker, and work has gone on slowly
and steadily as money allows over the last two decades. At the
chancel arch, what is revealed is a Doom of probably the late
thirteenth century, to which were added in the next 100 years a
Virgin, St John the Baptist and two censing angels. Later still, after
the Reformation, came a royal coat of arms. There is other
cartouche painting, notably the figure well preserved in the north-
east, a crowned head cocked inquiringly at the bauble he is holding
and begging, if not a question, then the cartoonist's bubble as a *coup
de grâce*.

All this is quite a jumble to unravel, and while these paintings
may not be major works of art, clearly they are deserving of the
utmost care. That such a small community should shoulder the
burden is immensely to its credit.

Castle Combe

WILTSHIRE
OS 173 842772
7 miles north-west of Chippenham

SOME WILL ARGUE that Castle Combe could never be Cotswold;
it is indeed peripheral, but in its setting, its cluster and its stone it
has so much of the Cotswold character that the indulgence is
impossible to deny. Set piece no doubt, self-conscious maybe, too
much tripped over, too often an obvious quarry for the film and
television people, disfigured alas by the inevitable parking arrangements – nevertheless, Castle Combe must still be one of the
loveliest villages in England.

The village is wonderfully situated in a gully, surrounded by
steep wooded hills (**54**). The combe is made by the By Brook as it
spills down off the Cotswold ridge between Bath and Stroud to the

Market Cross, Castle Combe

west, and comes bubbling, rushing past on its way to join the Avon near Bathford. From the bridge and its group of cottages, some rubblestone but mostly rendered, by the side of the brook, the street rises on a curve to the cross – a minor Malmesbury, sending its crocket and finial literally through the roof. It composes happily in almost any view within the village (**55**). Just beyond is perhaps the best house, the imposing Dower House (**55**) of about 1700; but imposing as it is, particularly with such relatively humble neighbours, its dignity would be better emphasized in ashlar than in roughcast. Its best feature is a remarkable shell-hood doorway.

There are blemishes. Just below the cross to the south there is some recent and ugly ribbon-pointing, broad bands of cement mortar trowelled on to the surface of the joints, sometimes an inch wide, and brought forward from the stone. The aesthetic effect is disastrous; and it can be unsound technically too, since the ledges of the projecting mortar can arrest the flow of rainwater down the wall and enable it to penetrate the stones behind. Ribbon-pointing always detracts from the natural beauty of stone; at worst it can appear as vertical crazy paving. Even humble rubblestone is deserving of a much more sensitive treatment. No wonder that on two of these cottages vegetation has been allowed vigorous play, a green laurel-like leaf on one, a harsh red cotoneaster on another. A splash of colour may look attractive on the postcards, but creepers are not a proper way to treat stone, even if they do disguise poor pointing.

[53]

Castle Combe

Next door, timbers, too black at that, are revealed; 'picturesque' perhaps, but out of place in limestone country.

Much of the church of St Andrew was rebuilt, and well, in the middle of the nineteenth century, although the stained glass makes it rather gloomy. The tower, Somerset-style with diagonal buttresses, is perhaps its most distinguished feature, and within it has a fan-vault and a soaring arch to the nave. To the north of the church a lane – with a delightful range of gabled cottages, a miniature Arlington Row (as at Bibury) – leads to the Manor House, now a

Castle Combe
Dower House, Castle Combe

hotel glorying in a view across well-manicured lawns to the ridge on the far side of the By Brook. The house dates from the seventeenth century, but received a lumpish though doubtless spacious west wing about 100 years ago. Nevertheless, it is a romantic spot, and specially relaxing for a break in winter or in early spring. That is the time to see Castle Combe: in the sun, but out of season, when even the bareness of the trees is an advantage with its revelation of distant views from the surrounding approaches.

Castle Eaton

WILTSHIRE
OS 163 146959
4 miles north-east of Cricklade

CASTLE EATON stands on the River Thames, about midway between Cricklade and Lechlade, only about fourteen miles from its source west of Cirencester. It is therefore a village of the plain, with rows of stone cottages, although at its northern approaches it has not escaped modern brick, concrete, cement, corrugated iron and tin. The church, somewhat quaint, is well sited by the side of the river; it was largely Victorianized in 1861–3 by Butterfield who added an odd-looking bell-turret precariously balanced on the ridge, and a spirelet. The best building in the village is the Red Lion, with a façade of hand-made Georgian brick – blues and reds used purely for aesthetic effect – and stone for the quoins, windows, and rear elevations. The house stands on a plinth of rubble-stone and has stone slates dutifully and beautifully graded at the roof. The dormers, casements without mullions, look a little bleak, and the symmetry has been adapted presumably to accommodate the entrance and to provide light for public rooms within. The effect is decidedly homespun, but the great pleasure is the unusual counterpoint of brick and stone: a match, it might be said, out of a misalliance.

The Red Lion, Castle Eaton

Chastleton

CHASTLETON IS IN a narrow neck of the extreme north-west corner of Oxfordshire where the county boundaries of Gloucestershire to the west and Warwickshire to the east are only just over a mile apart. There is not much of a village, but the church and large house form a memorable group. The church, dedicated to St Mary the Virgin, is a building of the late twelfth century enlarged two centuries later. It has a prominent but plain tower to the south, somewhat dumpy and of little interest. It was duly 'put into place' by the arrival of the Jacobean mansion adjacent, and the juxtaposition of church, house and gateway provide a setting of great attraction. Stables, a bakery and a brewhouse are to the west; the occasional cooing of doves in their eighteenth-century dovecot comes from the park just across the road.

The main front of the house faces south and is most satisfying. The stone is a glorious ashlar, in colour a mixture of golden brown and grey. The roof, which must surely be later, is of slate, but not aggressive, and luckily the harshness is mitigated by moss and lichen. There are two projecting square-angled bays running the whole height of the three storeys and the house has five gables on two planes. At either end, on yet again a different plane, is a robust and embattled staircase tower. The arrangement is entirely symmetrical and, as at Broughton, the effect is emphasized by the half-concealed front door.

The north front is plainer and flat, with the exception of a single central bay rising again through three storeys. The plan is rectangular around a small central court. Many of the inward-facing windows are blocked. The elevations are a little over-lofty, but their restraint, combined with the relationship of wall to window, is just right. Chastleton serves to reinforce the view that Jacobean architecture is attractive in inverse proportion to its ornateness; by comparison with the north front of Cecil's prodigious mansion at Hatfield in Hertfordshire, Chastleton proves the point with eloquence.

The architect is unknown; Robert Smythson, the great Elizabethan builder-architect of Hardwick and Wollaton, has been suggested, but Chastleton is altogether smaller and less ambitious. Mark Girouard, in a note provided by Jennifer Sherwood to her *Oxfordshire*, has proposed a possible link with Ralph Sheldon. He supplied the owner of the estate, Walter Jones, with the tapestries (somewhat faded and too full of allegorical figures) now on show in the house. Sheldon was related to Sir Henry Griffith who had employed Smythson for Burton Agnes.

Chastleton is usually on show at weekends from Easter to September, and has some fine rooms. On the first floor, in the north-east corner, is the Great Chamber, a well-proportioned room which provides a wealth of decoration. Fluted pilasters, blind arcading, strapwork, foliage and a frieze of caryatids crowd the scene, and above is a pendant ceiling. No expense has been spared;

this is a show of some extravagance. The Long Gallery occupies the whole of the north side. It is a panelled room, with three large windows overlooking the garden on the long side, and one at each end. It has a tunnel-vaulted ceiling, and a segmental arch adorned with strapwork and other rich embellishment. Much of the plaster-work in the house is of a style that appears in some of the Oxford colleges, and was perhaps worked by the same craftsmen.

The gardens are mainly grass, beautifully mown and well maintained, and there could be no more appropriate accompaniment to this lovely stone exterior. To the east is the Box Garden, laid out *c.*1700, a topiary with quaint clipped animals enclosing rose-beds. The house is best approached from the north, being strikingly placed on a hill at the boundary of the Cotswold ridge as it drops to the Vale of Evesham. Once seen, as the old cliché justifiably has it, never forgotten.

Chedworth

GLOUCESTERSHIRE
OS 163 053122
8 miles north-east of Cirencester

THE FAMOUS ROMAN VILLA to the north rather eclipses the village, strung out along the valley of a tributary of the River Coln. The former railway leaves a sad and occasionally ugly mark; devoid of their life-blood of steam and hiss, stumps of bridges and embankment mounds become a bit of a blot. Yet the village, large and straggling, has much to offer: a manor house, cottages, a barn dated 1785 at Cromwell House (one of two sizeable gabled houses of the seventeenth century), and an important church.

St Andrew, perfectly ashlared at the nave, looks to all the world on its southern side to be pure Perpendicular with its battlement, magnificent large windows and string of king-size gargoyles. This is all rather posh, but it is only a façade, the munificence of a late fifteenth-century wool merchant. Step inside, and the church is Norman, with chunky pillars, a great spreading arch between nave and tower, and a simple font. The treasure is the pulpit, Perpendicular and stone, the 'wineglass' model of Naunton, North Cerney and Cirencester, but Chedworth's is taller and the most graceful of the collection. In three places the church has dates in arabic numerals; 1485 low down on the turret at the south-east corner of the nave, 1461 (in roman as well) on the buttress east of the south porch, and 1491 on the jamb to the right of the south door. Roman numerals persist in Church and government until well into the 1700s. The Cotswold wool merchants here, as at Northleach, show that their trade and status knew wider horizons; they were international operators.

The Roman villa is beautifully situated under a canopy of trees in a wood, a mile away by footpath, or three along winding lanes for the motorist, often choked with traffic in the high season. Chedworth is a great favourite, and rightly so, with school parties. The museum ticket-office, neo-Tudor of 1870, does not suit the spirit of the place and today would be much more sensitively handled, but what the museum houses is excellent. There are over twenty sites of ROMAN VILLAS, intriguingly so marked on the map in the Cotswold area. Chedworth, *c*.AD 180–350, is the finest and most fully excavated. It was discovered dramatically in 1864 when Lord Eldon's gamekeeper, looking for a ferret, found a mosaic.

The villa is large and conveniently sited on a natural supply of clear spring-water and close to the Fosse Way. It must have belonged to a VIP, much given, as was the habit of Roman gentlemen, to bathing. He had both hot and dry baths, Turkish and sauna, and nearly all mod. cons.; living-, dining- and bedrooms, complete with underfloor heating. The mosaics resemble the Cirencester school, and geometric patterns predominate. The dining-room has the showpiece, figures of satyrs and nymphs, and the 'Winter' of the seasons, a peasant holding a rabbit – a long-lost ancestor, in spirit at least, of that Victorian gamekeeper.

Cherington

GLOUCESTERSHIRE
OS 163 903985
3½ miles north-east of Tetbury

THIS LITTLE VILLAGE, its charm often unnoticed, is set around the tiniest of greens and overlooks thick woods in the valley below. It has some Georgian cottages and a fine ashlar-faced farmhouse, Coxes by name, with bold detailing of keystones and quoins and a cast-iron veranda; and at Lowesmoor Farm, a mile or more to the north-east, there is a huge stone barn which has no fewer than seventeen bays, a kingpost roof, and a square tower on top. Cherington Park, just south of the church, is Georgian, somewhat

St Nicholas, Cherington

lacking in refinement, but solid and straightforward; two storeys, seven bays and a symmetrical front to the east. Over the side entrance is a Norman tympanum, a companion to the one over the north doorway of the church, whence it was presumably filched in a former 'restoration'. T. BALDWIN, CHURCHWARDEN an inscription over the church tympanum reads, CHURCH REPAIRED 1816. Perhaps the house benefited with its tympanum during the same reparations.

The church is small, well-kept, and much loved. The roof of the chancel is of stone, although that of the nave is of lead. The churchyard is marred by one grey granite cross, out of keeping with the stone tomb-chests that otherwise grace this quiet spot. The bronze plaque has disappeared, spirited away perhaps in retribution. Within the church, restored in the 1880s, there is not much to see, but the Early English chancel remains complete and virtually unspoiled. Georgian communion rails with turned balusters protect the altar, and the lancets and quatrefoil of the east window make an agreeable composition. A fine arch frames this sanctuary of calm (**59**).

Chipping Campden
GLOUCESTERSHIRE
OS 151 155395
8 miles north-west of
Moreton-in-Marsh

CHIPPING CAMPDEN is among the most famous of all Cotswold attractions. Scarcely one false note intrudes; it is packed full of splendid architecture. Packed full of visitors, too, on a sunny day in high summer, and amidst such bustle it is hard to imagine that in 1836 the Cotswold parson, the Revd F. E. Witts, could write that 'Campden is a dull, clean, disused market town'.

From the fourteenth to the seventeenth century Chipping Campden was the regional centre of the wool trade, England's chief export, and there was a weekly market here and three fair days each year as early as 1247. Chipping, or 'Chepying', as at Chipping Norton, and again at Tetbury, means a market, and derives from the Old English *cēping*. Not many of the existing houses are medieval but one that is particularly unspoiled is the house of William Grevel (**61**), which dates from about 1400. Grevel was rich and famous, 'the flower', as his tomb in the parish church records, 'of the wool merchants of all England'. His fortune was made not always scrupulously, if we are to believe a hint on a tax roll of 1380 that he and his son had been pardoned 'for all unjust and excessive weighings and purchase of wool contrary to the statute'. Successful entrepreneurs or sour grapes?

His house is built of rubblestone, although that would have been distinguished enough in a street of wattle and daub. The bay window, however, in ashlar, is a gem, shallow in projection but with verticals that give an impression of great height, and moulded and carved stonework of great dignity. The panelling and the six cinquefoil-headed lights are especially attractive, and two large gargoyles glower from above. The roof has limestone slates, rich in texture and beautifully graded; both the

Grevel House, Chipping Campden

Almshouses, Chipping Campden

chimney-piece and the arch are contemporary with the house.

Grevel built his house in the main street of the town; a handsome street with wide verges fringed with trees, and it gains enormously from its graceful curve. There is a fine array of houses of different dates; at the Martins (**64**) the seventeenth and eighteenth century are juxtaposed. Little Martins with its gables and mullions is the earlier, while The Martins has a date of 1714. This house looks suspiciously as if it might hide an earlier construction; it looks decidedly rustic, though none the less charming for that, and the short fluted Ionic pilasters at the first storey seem very much an afterthought. The glazing is by no means all of a piece or a period, and the stone, with a jumbly patch below the ground-floor windows, is mostly ashlar, of more pretentious workmanship and coursing than next door.

Five centuries are represented along this happily snapped High Street, and wherever you look there is much to attract the eye and raise the spirit. The shortest of lists must include Woolstaplers' Hall, contemporary with Grevel but built for Robert Calf, another successful wool merchant. He too got an oriel window, an impressive oak roof within, and a fireplace with his family rebus, too easy and obvious an opportunity to miss. Dovers House is a Georgian building, gracious and well-proportioned, and the Regency Cotswold House Hotel offers comfortable hospitality behind finely detailed ashlar.

St James, Chipping Campden

Jacobean conduit, Chipping Campden

Woolstaplers' Hall was restored by C. R. Ashbee, apostle of the Arts and Crafts, who did much work in the town and who in 1902 moved his Guild of Handicrafts into the Silk Mill in Sheep Street. Twenty-seven years later, F. L. Griggs, in the same tradition, formed the Campden Trust which has since collaborated closely with the National Trust. Conservation has been Chipping Campden's constant guide, and the National Trust has in its excellent care the Market Hall, erected in 1627 and apparently intended for the sale of cheese, butter and poultry. The donor was Sir Baptist Hicks, who used his wool fortune in great benefactions to the town. His coat of arms appears at one end of his Market Hall, under an ogee gable.

Sir Baptist also gave the town the almshouses (**62**) and even provided them with a water supply from a sturdy little conduit beside the road half a mile to the south on Westington Hill. The almshouses, close by the church, date from about 1612, and were built at a cost of £1,300. They form an 'I' (Iacobus) for James I, and

The Martins and Little Martins,
Chipping Campden

are exquisite; twelve small houses, each pair with a four-centred arch and moulded outer door. The upper windows all have finely designed hood-moulds, the gables delicate coping and decorative finials. The stone is a striking colour, a mixture of cream and grey, spotted here and there with silver-grey lichen. Above all is the rippling texture of the stone roof; when this roof was stripped for repair some thirty years ago, about half these slates, laid in 1612, were still perfectly sound.

Closing this vista to the east, and commanding the entrance to the town from an eminence, stands the church of St James (**63**), and beside it to the south the lodges, gateway and pavilions of the old manor, built by Sir Baptist in 1613, and burned down by the occupants in preference to surrendering it to Cromwell. What is left was repaired on the advice of F. L. Griggs about 1930. The church was originally Norman, and was transformed, if ever words could be more truly said, 'on the backs of sheep' in the fifteenth century. The tower is the great status symbol, stylish and stately. It is best seen from the south-east, and the model was Gloucester Cathedral, just as Wells was for so many of the Somerset towers. It dates from about 1450 and is a typical Gloucestershire creation, but with one unusual detail, the subsidiary pinnacles which spring from ogee arches in front of the parapet. The buttress in front of the west window is unfortunate and detracts from the impact of the otherwise splendid proportions and parapet.

Within, the style is entirely Perpendicular, the effect light and airy, the masoncraft superb. The nave is lofty with a soaring tower arch and there is a large window over the chancel arch, a Cotswold speciality. The plaster on the walls is colour-washed in cream to tone with the stone. The piers of the nave, octagonal with concave sides, are not moulded but scalloped, unusual and decorative; they are so similar to Northleach that this arcade must be by the same hand. The arches are a little flat, four-centred but not in the customary manner, and the piers seem by way of compensation rather tall. The roofs in the aisles are a little disappointing, and in the nave they are flat, dull and too brown. Only in the choir is the roof at all remarkable: robust, cambered and tie-beamed, grey-brown in colour, but plain.

The glass is luckily mostly clear. The east window is by Henry Payne of Amberley in Gloucestershire, 1925; it is not bad at a distance, and there are some fragments of medieval glass incorporated within it, but on close inspection it palls. Otherwise the nineteenth-century glass is weak, or worse. There are, however, some noble monuments in the Hicks Chapel. Sir Baptist, who also gave the church its pulpit and lectern, died in 1629. He was ennobled as Lord Campden, which name, incidentally, he gave to his house and indeed a whole enclave in Kensington, West London. He lies with his wife, formidable of feature, an old battleaxe if looks are anything to go by. The sculpture is of high quality, perhaps by Nicholas Stone or Francesco Fanelli. Their son and daughter-in-law are commemorated close by in a monument signed by Joshua Marshall. Both monuments are sumptuous, but black and white marble and alabaster look out of place amongst the glowing oolitic limestone ashlar of the rest of the church.

There are some exceptionally fine brasses, the earliest and largest, five feet two and a half inches, being to William Grevel, who died in 1401, and his wife. There are medieval textiles on show: an early fifteenth-century velvet cope, good to see but in poor condition, and white silk altar frontals, well preserved but interesting mainly as survivors from about 1500. The chapel at the end of the north aisle has some pleasant modern silver, including candlesticks and a cross made at the Guild by George Hart. There is some wood-carving, communion rails and panelling, and an altar together with three screens, all in oak, designed by Norman Jewson in the 1950s.

In Chipping Campden the stone is a particularly beautiful golden oolite from Westington quarry just a mile up the hill to the south-west. As a collection of buildings the town is nothing grand, but has everything just right, homogeneous and neighbourly. With Burford in the Oxfordshire Cotswolds, it is in a class of its own.

Chipping Norton

OXFORDSHIRE
OS 164 313271
12 miles south-west of Banbury

St Mary, Chipping Norton ▷

THE CHARM OF CHIPPING NORTON lies in its setting on a hill, with different levels, steps, streets and houses spilling gently down to the valley below. The approach from the west is dominated by the Bliss Valley Tweed Mill (**69**). It is a handsome building, well sited and well seen from both the roads to Evesham and Stow-on-the-Wold. It stands by what used to be the railway that meandered delightfully through the Cotswolds and linked the two arms of the Great Western at King's Sutton in the east and Cheltenham to the west. With its parapet, balustrade and corner towers, the building could have passed for a mansion set in a park, were it not for its soaring chimney-stack. The mill would look quite at home in the Pennines, and is indeed the work of George Woodhouse who hailed from Lancashire. It is dated 1872.

The mill is a reminder that Chipping Norton had a manufacturing life well into recent times and is still a bustling market town. There is particular evidence of prosperity in the eighteenth century, when many of the earlier houses were refronted to provide fashionable façades (**68**). Hotels and inns often led the way; one example is the White Hart Hotel in the High Street, in a yellowy ashlar, and the Bunch of Grapes opposite in Middle Row, gabled and in coursed rubblestone, also had alterations at that time. The White Hart is baroque in feeling, and the former King's Head in New Street, identifiable by its carriage entrance and now converted into

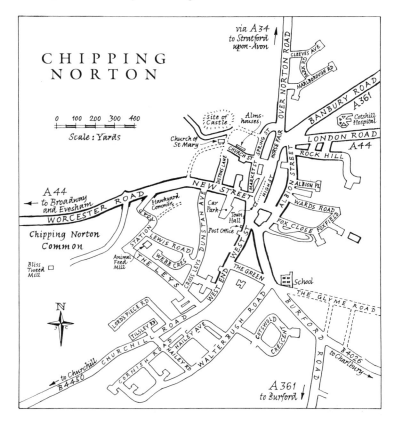

High Street, Chipping Norton

flats, is decidedly Vanbrughian in style, with giant pilasters rising the height of the façade. Much of this building of *c*.1730 would, it seems, have been influenced by the work of Vanbrugh at Blenheim twelve miles to the south-east.

The Town Hall, dated 1842, is by G. S. Repton, the fourth and youngest son of Humphrey Repton. In his youth he worked with his father and also in John Nash's office before launching on a career designing country houses, mostly in the West. His Town Hall is solid, sober and well-mannered. Church Lane leads down a hill off to the west to the church, and here stand the almshouses (**69**), an attractive row of eight gables and nine chimney-stacks dating from 1640.

At the bottom of the valley, immediately to the south of the earthworks of what must have been a sizeable castle, is the church of St Mary (**67**). It is built of a pleasant stone but with some yellow patching, and its most striking feature is a fine hexagonal south porch, one of only three of the type in England. It has two storeys with a parapet and gargoyles and some devilish bosses at the vault (**69**). Within there is a high Perpendicular nave, rebuilt *c*.1485, bearing comparison with Northleach, Cirencester and Fairford. It has thin moulded piers and stone panelling but is marred by a poor roof. There are two aisles to the north and one to the south; this is a wide 'town' church with pews for several hundred. The clerestory should provide an almost continuous resplendent lantern light, but it has disappointing pink and blueish glass.

The chancel is low, dark and dull, but at the east end of the south aisle, which dates from the early Decorated building, is a window of splendid flowing tracery. It is of six lights with a wheel at the top, and is said to have come from Bruern Abbey at the Dissolution; the nineteenth-century glass does it no disservice. There is a series of brasses, somewhat mutilated, set up on wooden panels in the north aisle, and two sixteenth-century table tombs of note, each with two effigies in alabaster: one to Richard Croft and his wife, near the organ, the other to Thomas Rickardes and his spouse. St Mary's has its moments, but architecturally it is somehow not quite as satisfying as one might expect from so distinguished an exterior.

△ Almshouses, Chipping Norton

Bliss Valley Tweed Mill, ▷
Chipping Norton

▽ Boss in south porch, St Mary,
Chipping Norton

St John the Baptist and Market Place, Cirencester

Cirencester

DESPITE ALL THE PRESSURES of the present century, Cirencester remains at heart unspoilt, the self-proclaimed capital of the Cotswolds, an example of English town architecture at its best. It stands on the River Churn, a small tributary of the upper Thames. Standing in the market-place before the grandiloquent porch of the parish church, it is timely to reflect that here is a town that has known two millennia of history. Cirencester was an early headquarters of the Second Legion, and under Diocletian became the capital of Britannia Prima, one of the four provinces of Roman Britain, being second in size only to Londinium.

The town was strategically sited at the junction of four Roman roads, long stretches of which still run (almost) straight for miles across the surrounding country. The forum stood at the intersection of Ermine Street, on its route from Winchester north-west to Gloucester, and the Fosse Way, which leads from Exeter and Bath across the Midlands to Lincoln. A fifth road, Akeman Street, branching eastwards to Bicester and Colchester, is only a mile away. Cester, chester and caster all derive from the Roman word *castrum*, and it seems that Cirencester owes its name to the fort of the Cornovii, a tribe whose territory was not far to the north. John Leland, writing about 1540, said the name had been shortened to Cicestre; about 1725 Defoe wrote 'Ciciter for brevity'. A hundred years later Cobbett noted that 'local people call it Cititer'. In the 1940s I remember my father cycling to 'Cicester' (sisister), but locals now shorten the name to Ciren.

The Roman town was laid out on the customary grid plan but not much of this survives, and the narrow winding lanes of the medieval town, north and west of the church, contain all the best architecture and are much more visually rewarding. However, there are some important Roman remains, one of the best collections of Roman antiquities in Britain, well housed and displayed in the Corinium Museum in Park Street. The treasures include a Corinthian capital, an imposing piece of public sculpture only discovered in 1838, and in all probability carved from local limestone quarried near the amphitheatre just outside the town to the south-west. There are also some excellent floor mosaics, great status-symbols for the private citizen. The best of these depict hunting-dogs in full pursuit of their quarry (which is alas missing), and a hare, which was found on an allotment as recently as 1971. The material used for these mosaics was almost entirely stone, tiny cubes of different colours about half an inch square known as tesserae, carefully bedded into cement and polished.

The church of St John, with its tower 160 feet high – the tallest of any parish church in Gloucestershire – dominates the centre of the town and many of the views along the streets around (**70**). There was previously an Augustinian abbey, which though rich was no friend of the town and opposed its attempts to obtain borough privileges; the proud tower of the parish church, built by

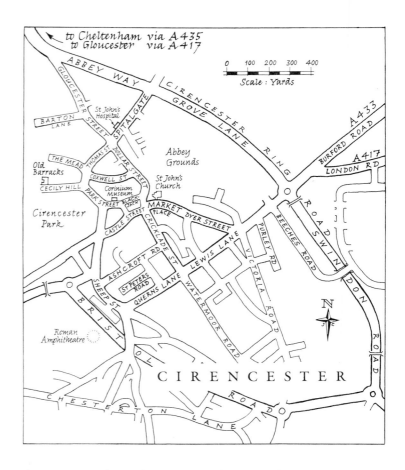

the townspeople on the proceeds of rewards for loyalty to Henry IV against the deposed Richard II, is a symbol of their determination to assert their independence of the abbey. It was begun about 1400 on the site of a filled-in ditch running alongside Ermine Street. The foundations were not firm and soon began to settle; large buttresses had to be built to support it and a projected spire was abandoned. In its place was added a broad band which interrupts the tower's upward thrust, and the short top stage, although it has a delicate pierced parapet with finials, comes somewhat as an afterthought.

The south porch, however, is a triumph (**73**). No other parish church has a porch three storeys high, and with its oriel windows and profusion of panelling it is the most magnificent in the county. It was built after the tower about 1490 as an office, surprisingly enough by the abbey which controlled the market and much of the surrounding land. Between 1671 and 1897 the upper chamber served as the town hall.

The most striking feature of the church interior is the lofty arcade, whose effect is reinforced by the graceful slenderness of the piers and the height of the clerestory. All around, solid walls have dissolved into glass. The soaring tower arch at the west has an

South porch, St John the Baptist, ▷
Cirencester

attractive lierne vault, but the best feature of the church is the fan vault, crisp and confidently carved, in St Catharine's Chapel, north of the chancel. It dates from 1508. The stone pulpit, part of it discreetly coloured, is one of only a few from before the Reformation to have escaped unscathed, and takes the form of a wineglass on a delicate stem, the toast no doubt of many a sermon's end.

In the Trinity Chapel are some memorable brasses, mostly dating from the fifteenth century, commemorating wool merchants, one of whom, the prolific Robert Page, had only one wife, but six sons and eight daughters. The church's special treasure is the exquisite Boleyn cup, gilt and hallmarked 1535, on show at the side of the entrance to the chancel in a glass-fronted wall case. This church is big and somewhat shapeless, and the impression is not helped by a whole regiment of unattractive pews, unrelentingly lined up and, one fears, all too sparsely peopled on Sundays. On a sunny day the clear windows admit a brilliant light, but elsewhere there is fairly indifferent stained glass. A mere taste of a rather pallid pre-Reformation glass was rescued and assembled in 1929 by F. C. Eden in a small two-light window in the south sanctuary wall above the sedilia. It was found in a crate, the only survivor from a number, containing unwanted fragments from an eighteenth-century restoration, which were tipped into a ditch beside the Cirencester–Kemble railway line in 1890.

To the north of the church was the abbey. Of the abbey church, half as long again as the parish's although not as wide, nothing remains; but the grounds, for centuries in the ownership of a private house now demolished, were bought by the town in 1965. They make a spacious recreational area, a vast lawn bordered to the east by the quiet waters of the River Churn. A walk by the river brings you to the abbey's north gate, a Norman arch devoid of ornament to either side, with walls of local rubblestone. It has a steep pitched roof, clad in graded stone slates.

An ordered exploration begins and ends at the market-place, whose shape is interesting and unusual – concave to the north, with a gentle and continuing curve to the east. It is now cluttered with parked cars, and how one yearns for it to be restored as an open space, cobbled, paved or with hoggin. The fascias on the shops leave a great deal to be desired and are generally undistinguished. What a pity it is that commercial enterprise does not respect public good taste more, and that planning authorities, especially in the conservation areas, do not exert more rigorous control. None the less there is a pleasing and mixed array of buildings; to the north a 'chorus of jolly painted stucco', as Alec Clifton-Taylor* so characteristically described it, 'sings happily and harmoniously on Georgian fronts which often hide an earlier building behind'. From the churchyard, numbers 9 to 17 show that at the back they are really

*Another Six English Towns, BBC, 1984. Cirencester was the first programme in a BBC TV series of the same title which this book accompanied.

Dollar Street, Cirencester ▷

all one house. Some of these houses are Stuart or even Tudor, but only one, the Fleece Hotel, reveals its timber frame. It looks out of place amongst all the stone and stucco, and some of the timbers have been blackened while many others, on close inspection, are a sham, only painted stucco. Such is the pull of the 'quaint' look, however, that a few years ago the other half of this hotel, a decent Georgian façade, was given the same bogus treatment. The excellent Civic Society saw to it that this was promptly and properly removed. To the south the buildings are later, larger and stone-faced, with a fair expanse of sheet-glass windows. The most prominent and indeed the most attractive is the Corn Exchange, in a fine quality limestone with carved masks on the keystones, and a delightful musical motif in the tympanum. For those with a head for heights, a climb to the top of the church tower is well worth while; the shape of the town is well seen, together with a medley of roofs, slate, concrete, and all too few of stone.

Let us strike north. The road follows the line of the abbey wall, and against it numbers 2 to 8 Dollar Street are a row of seventeenth-century cottages with gables. Two of them are now dressed in boudoir pink, already a little faded, but too effeminate and out of place in the street scene; much better in my lady's chamber. Dollar Street (75) has no transatlantic connections, nor is it anything to do with the 'dolours' or griefs or miseries that town guides sometimes invite visitors to associate with plague ditches. Its derivation is the dole, a pittance then as now, and dispensed in medieval days from the Dole Hall or almonry of the abbey. As the street develops there is a show of impressive ashlar to right and left and the junction with Spitalgate invites a strategic pause. In Spitalgate itself is St John's Hospital (77), a fragment of medieval Cirencester, founded by Henry II. Four bays of the hall arcade survive, worthily restored in a rubbly stone, while a fifth to the west incorporates a cottage. At the entrance to Gloucester Street is the Rebecca Powell School, long to the street with windows at the first floor keeping their original leaded panes, and seven dormers lighting the attic. The narrow side elevation has a roundel, a window and a door set in formidable rustication. Gloucester Street retains more of pre-Georgian Cirencester than any other, with gables and overhangs jostling on a curve, always visually inviting. Numbers 33 to 35 are of special note, a sixteenth-century timber-framed cottage standing on a plinth of large ashlar blocks of stone, which must have come from the abbey shortly after the Dissolution. The cement render and the slate roof are not attractive, nor is the brown paint, of all colours, at the White Lion opposite, but this is a street to wander and enjoy.

Much else that should be seen lies conveniently arranged in a segment bordered by Thomas Street, Park Street and Black Jack Street (which leads back to the market-place), with a spur off to the west at Cecily Hill. In Thomas Street, first comes St Thomas's

St John's Hospital, Spitalgate, ▷
Cirencester

[76]

Hospital (**79**), founded in the early fifteenth century and perhaps the oldest domestic building in the town, rubbly and medieval in its gait, with small rectangular windows low down and high up, save one understandably altered a couple of centuries later to admit more light below. Over the low four-centred arch of the doorway is a poor, defaced, scarcely readable image. This hospital became known as Weavers' Hall, which gives a clue to Cirencester's medieval prosperity. There were about ten million sheep in medieval England, and half a million, a special breed with a long, heavy fleece, grazed the Cotswolds. Many of the grander houses in the town, even after the wool trade had moved elsewhere, must have been owned by clothiers and wool merchants.

Thomas Street has its share of attractive eighteenth-century architecture, particularly at Mead House, number 20, and the nearby Old Vicarage, perhaps the most distinguished in the collection. There are similarities in design between these two, although the ashlar of the former vicarage wins hands down over the render of its neighbour. Further along the street is Monmouth House, a Tudor reworking of a house built much earlier. It is a beguiling mixture of trefoil windows and flat arches at the entrance, and first-floor windows which have hooded dripmoulds with decorated stops.

Arched dripmoulds, Thomas Street, Cirencester

St Thomas's Hospital, Thomas Street, ▷ Cirencester

Rubblestone house, Thomas Street, Cirencester

Next door at the junction with Cecily Hill is a detached house of five bays, sashed at least at the first storey in the correct Georgian fashion; but the ground floor lacks symmetry, and the windows here bump against the line of what looks suspiciously like a seventeenth-century timber-framed jetty or overhang. At some time it seems to have been divided into two, or to have had a passage inserted at the side. The stone is coursed rubble, rustic in appearance, and the roof has small, carefully graded stone slates. The dormers have frilly Victorian bargeboards. This house undoubtedly wears its history on its sleeve, but with some careful reordering at ground level could make more of its pretensions. It enjoys a good position, and is luckily set back from the swirling traffic of the one-way flow at the garden gate.

Nearly opposite, at 27 Park Street, is another building seeking to mask seventeenth-century origins, Dunstall House. The doorway, moulded stone architraves, oval windows (half-obscured by the pavement) and excellent quoins proclaim Georgian. For this to be true, however, the proportion of the windows, always a tell-tale, would be quite different: four lights up by three across, not four by four as here; and although the glazing dates from the eighteenth century, it cannot disguise the original window arrangement, which would have been casements and leaded lights.

Opposite Dunstall House is one of the most extraordinary sights of England: an enormous semicircular yew hedge, forty-two feet high, twelve feet wide at the top and broader at the base. It is enclosed by a rubblestone wall which scarcely rises to half its height, and prefaced by a gateway which expresses its strong if somewhat eccentric personality in chunky and for the most part uncoursed rubblestone, with rusticated ashlar for the quoins and quasi-Gibbs surround of the round-arched doorway, the whole

Park Street, Cirencester

being topped by a cornice and three finial balls. Unless you had climbed the church tower, which offers the only view, you would be unaware that behind all this lies Cirencester House, the town's only mansion. If this enclosure was not such an oddity it might seem a little unfriendly, shutting out the town as at Petworth in Sussex; but a Georgian weather vane rises above the lead-capped cupola of the stables (**81**) and tells of life beyond the hedge.

The house and its park were the creation of Allen, the first Lord Bathurst, between 1714 and 1718. The earl was an unswerving Tory (he owed his title to his mother's close friendship with Queen Anne) and the best architect of his day, James Gibbs, was in the pocket of the Whigs, so Bathurst had to make do with a local mason. The house, while imposing, is therefore architecturally rather a plain Jane, and perhaps understandably shy behind its yew.

The park is approached from Cecily Hill, the town's most elegant street, broad and well proportioned with a gradient – narrow at the lower end and widening beyond – which enhances the impression of its length. The buildings, as elsewhere in Cirencester, all give much pleasure, but are not markedly superior, and rubblestone, quite often roughly hewn, is much in evidence; a smooth ashlar would have given a more urbane and stylish appearance. A most distinguished example of rubblestone is number 32, early Georgian, symmetrical, correct in proportions with pediment and cornice, and displaying the original handmade crown glass in its windows (**83**). Number 5, a Queen Anne house, has a bay window in brick with Gothick tracery, out of keeping but no less attractive for that, but the least expected building of all is the Old Barracks, formerly the armoury of the Royal North Gloucestershire Militia, built in 1857. It is every small boy's dream, a complete toy fort, gatehouse, battlements, lancets, drum tower, and an octagonal stair turret, battlemented and machicolated. In every detail, in conformity with Victorian practice, it is asymmetrical, and it seems only to lack drawbridge and portcullis. The militia have marched away into history, and the town band, who once appropriately made this their headquarters, plays on now elsewhere. At the top of Cecily Hill a superb Georgian screen, with delicate wrought-iron overthrow, marks the entrance to Cirencester Park.

The people of Cirencester owe Lord Bathurst a great debt, for this must be one of the most valuable assets of any town in England – an immense open space, unspoiled and untrammelled, on its very doorstep, freely and generously accessible to the pedestrian, but thankfully not to wheeled traffic. It measures over 10,000 acres, laid out in the French style with straight avenues converging on *ronds-points*; at one point no fewer than ten avenues meet. Broad Avenue, grandest of all, runs in a straight line for over four miles nearly all the way to Sapperton. On either side of this wonderful ride are beech and horse-chestnut, and elsewhere oak and elm (where they have survived the ravages of the recent disease), yew and conifer. The planting, lavish and enthusiastic, is historically of interest, since this was the last of the great parks created before landscape in the style of Capability Brown became the fashion.

The noble lord commissioned a romantic but rather undistinguished group of 'ornaments', among them Alfred's Hall, the first castellated folly in England, and Ivy Lodge, with central tower, gabled ends and Gothick windows. In addition there is a round tower, a square house, a hexagon, an artificial lake, an obelisk, and Pope's Seat, named after the poet and garden designer who had influenced Stourhead in Wiltshire and with whom Bathurst collaborated at Cirencester. Queen Anne, set up as an act of piety in 1741 atop a Doric column on an axis from the church tower

32, Cecily Hill, Cirencester

through the centre of the mansion, surveys the scene. All is well; this is a park to explore at will.

Coxwell Street is the best route back to the town centre. It is a narrow street, crowded with outstanding architecture, which can scarcely have changed in centuries. Double yellow lines, always a disfigurement, nevertheless keep it mercifully and almost unfailingly clear of parked vehicles, and the pedestrian can generally enjoy a quiet and unencumbered walk back to the market-place. Number 51 is a fine Stuart building, ashlared throughout, and its neighbour at the corner with Thomas Street is Woolgatherers, historically one of the more interesting houses in town. It is seventeenth-century in origin, with a Jacobean staircase within and some panelled rooms which date from Queen Anne. Only the second-floor windows retain their original character, casements with leaded lights; at the ground floor they have been sashed, with thick glazing bars revealing an early date. Aesthetically, these windows would look more convincing with a ratio of three lights to five, not six. This eighteenth-century facelift, with its ashlared doorcase, was no doubt intended to give its resident clothier a house more in keeping with his dignity. To the left, enclosing an open courtyard, is his counting-house, single-storey and rather clumsily pushed up against the main façade; to the right, much higher, rendered and unfortunately pink at the ground floor, is extended living accommodation. This addition overlooks Thomas Street; it has a large Venetian window and next door to it a fine warehouse, balanced by a similar Venetian window beyond. The windows are rather messy and many are blocked, but this could be a most attractive elevation and welcome presence in the town.

Cirencester escaped the Industrial Revolution. The cloth trade declined, farming flourished, and the market became the town's focus. Wedged in between the two great estates of the abbey and the park, the historic core could not expand, and remains tightly knit. The main railway line passed to the west, leaving the town, eighteen miles equidistant from Cheltenham and Gloucester, and even further from Swindon, to enjoy a life of its own. A ring road, with its usual flotsam and jetsam, routes much of the through traffic away from the conservation area; car parks are tucked away and none is multi-storeyed. Cirencester seems to be in safe hands. It needs more ashlar and less rubble to be in the absolute top flight of English towns, but it is a splendid place to visit.

Cogges

OXFORDSHIRE
OS 164 362095
½ a mile east of Witney

Thirteenth-century lancet,
The Vicarage, Cogges

COGGES (pronounced Coggs) is best approached on foot, by a path which begins near the Butter Cross in Witney and crosses two streams of the River Windrush, and the meadows in between (**86**). The church, parsonage, and manor house with its outbuildings, sympathetically and cleverly restored as a farm museum by the county council,* form a striking group which still has a strong medieval aura. The manor house dates partly from the thirteenth century. It is well laid out with traditional farmhouse furnishings and kitchen implements, and gives a vivid impression of how life might have been led here until the First World War. It is L-shaped in plan, and the south wall of the medieval hall which is the core of the house retains two Early English two-light windows of *c.*1250. The original building was altered in the sixteenth century and raised in height to include an inserted floor. The masonry is rubble with dressings of ashlar, and the three-storey wing added to the east in the seventeenth century is for the most part covered in stucco.

The farmyard is the setting for a display of pieces of farm equipment mostly dating from the nineteenth century. The barns are nearly all roofed in stone, although there are also some thatch and tile. The manor was settled by the time of Domesday, and its moats, formerly fed by the streams of the Windrush but now dry, still exist. A village grew up to farm the surrounding fields to the south and east and a small Benedictine priory, colonized by the monks of Fécamp in Normandy, was founded in 1103.

Their priory house has been in clerical possession of one sort or another for eight centuries. Even after the Dissolution, when King Henry VIII granted the manor to Eton College, part of the house was reserved as the chaplain's residence by the gentry tenants who took on responsibility for the ministry of the church. In 1859 it was repossessed by the diocese of Oxford as the vicarage. It was, characteristically, considered too small for the incoming vicar and his family, and G. E. Street expanded it with a wing to the east. He confidently changed all the seventeenth-century fenestration of the existing building to match his new creation, bleak and boringly Victorian, but in so doing he unblocked the narrow thirteenth-century lancet which lit the original medieval hall.

It is divided at the top by the insertion of a floor within to make two levels of accommodation, perhaps for the parochial priest, in what was hitherto a large space open to the roof. The window looks somewhat incongruous now in the façade, but it has a tall and

*The pleasure of a visit to Cogges is greatly enhanced by the excellent guide published by the Cogges Agricultural Heritage Museum Association Ltd and produced by the Museum Services Department of the Oxfordshire County Council. It is edited by John M. Steane. For the archaeologically inclined there is a most informative article, 'Investigations at Cogges, 1978–81: the Priory and Parish Church', by John Blair and John M. Steane, in *Oxoniensia*, vol. XLVII (1982), published by the Oxfordshire Architectural Historical Society.

Cogges, Oxfordshire

slender charm, and a tale to tell. It was most fortunate that more recently when the Vicarage was considered too large, the diocese did not rehouse its vicar in a new suburban house, but let him stay in the old part, and sold off the Victorian wing. The barn, further east, once a school, is about to become a parish centre.

The church of St Mary is nearly square in shape. The stone is a white-grey at the west end which is part of the earliest Norman building, and here, placed diagonally in the north aisle, rises the tower, something of an oddity – square at ground level but octagonal at the next two stages and surmounted by a pyramid roof (**87**). The church, because of its Fécamp connections, shows a strong French influence. This is particularly evident in the north chapel, a flamboyant addition of the mid-fourteenth century with

St Mary and the Vicarage, ▷
Cogges

some fine reticulated tracery at the east window, and carved ornament of rosettes and ballflower at the windows and rere-arches. The stone cornice has a lively band of half-humans, half-animals, making no end of a racket with their viol, dulcimer, harp, bagpipes, tabor and pipe. There are two memorable monuments. The effigy of a lady, perhaps Margaret de Grey, of the family who owned the manor *c.*1350, lies on a chest carved at the sides with the emblems of the Evangelists within foiled circles. Three marble busts commemorate William Blake, a later owner, his wife Sarah and son Francis, the lady *décolletée* and the gentlemen in wigs.

Coln Rogers

GLOUCESTERSHIRE
OS 163 088096
5 miles south-west of Northleach

THE RIVER COLN gives its name to three villages: Coln Rogers and Coln St Dennis above Bibury, and Coln St Aldwyns, four miles north of Fairford. Coln Rogers is remarkable primarily for the church of St Andrew, an almost complete Saxon nave and chancel. The stone, suitable for its age and rural setting, is rubble, roughly coursed but dressed with smoother blocks. Long-and-short work, the Saxon tell-tale, can be seen at all corners of the nave save the north-east, and added clues are pilaster strips and the minute north window in the chancel, which is unaligned and 'weeps' to the south. Shortly after the Conquest the church was passed to the abbey of Gloucester by Roger de Gloucester who gave the village its name. The south doorway, with its plain tympanum, dates from this period. The font also is Norman. There is a fine old medieval oak chest with its original ironwork, but the interior is marred by gloomy glass and Victorian pews, out of scale with the size and simplicity of the church.

Coln St Dennis

OS 163 086109

AT COLN ST DENNIS, a mile upstream to the north, the church is Norman and dedicated to St James, but is recorded in Domesday as in the ownership of the parish church of St Denis from whom the village took its name and misguidedly added an 'n' over the centuries. The church retains its Norman plan, with an aisleless nave, a short sanctuary, and a central tower which carries a Perpendicular upper stage, too small in proportion. There are some amusing Norman grotesques, set on corbel heads to carry the original roof, and a good collection of memorial tablets. The Rectory of about 1810 is stucco and has acquired a slate roof. The architect was Richard Pace, a builder from Lechlade, who with his son built a number of parsonages in the Fairford district. Their work is only known from a trade card, which they issued in 1830, showing engravings of twenty-seven buildings, but, says H. M. Colvin,* it is evidence 'not wholly to be trusted'.

Coln St Aldwyns

OS 163 144053

COLN ST ALDWYNS is said to take its name from the hermit St Ealdwine. It lies seven or eight miles to the south-east, on the fringe of a deer park beside an old manor house, Elizabethan in origin but restored, altered and roughcast over the centuries. In the grounds is a dovecot, square and built of rubble with four gables and a lantern. Williamstrip Park, square and Georgian, is to the east. The lodge, built in 1822 in the Gothick manner, is listed on Richard Pace's trade card. The village is attractively laid out round the green, sandwiched between these two estates. The church, dedicated to St John the Baptist, is essentially Norman, and belonged, like Coln Rogers, to Gloucester Abbey until the Dissolution. It retains its ancient south door, and just to the west is the figure of a ferocious demon in hot pursuit of a man whose hand he is already about to

*A Biographical Dictionary of British Architects 1600–1840, John Murray, 1978.

devour. John Keble was curate to his father here from 1825 to 1835, but as there was no suitable vicarage they lived at Fairford. The church was cruelly restored in 1853. The classically inclined might dally at the font deciphering a Greek palindrome, but the only redeeming feature artistically is the chandelier of *c.*1767, an admirable piece of craftsmanship from Bristol.

Cornwell

OXFORDSHIRE
OS 163 273272
3½ miles west of Chipping Norton

THE VILLAGE is half a mile from the Gloucestershire border and lies in a combe above a stream which drains into the River Evenlode to the west. All the cottages are stone and roofed with stone, save one with thatch. The village was almost completely reconditioned in 1938–9 by Clough Williams Ellis, the eccentric and eclectic architect of Portmeirion in North Wales, and *inter alia* he enclosed the village green with a stone wall. It is all rather precious and private; no entry, we are advised, is allowed for motor vehicles, equestrians or pedestrians, except for access. The village hall, formerly the school, is neo-Georgian but with an apse at one end which has tall narrow windows in the style of Queen Anne. It has a hipped roof of Stonesfield stone slates, and an odd bellcote which appears to double as a chimney-stack. It is all a bit of a muddle, but the notice-defying trespasser who dares essay the cobblestones and the splash of the ford nearby will find charm and the picturesque.

The manor house, behind the village to the east, is Jacobean in origin, gabled and irregular, but the south and east fronts were refaced *c.*1750 in the classical style of the period. The stone is coursed and dressed rubblestone of a fawn colour with touches of grey. It is L-shaped with lower ranges to the west and north added by Clough Williams Ellis, and from this direction, glimpsed from a footpath through a field to the church, a fascinating roofscape emerges revealing the earlier building. There is also a fine vista, directly in line with the south front of the house, which can be seen from a gateway a little way along the road to Chipping Norton.

The little church of St Peter, built of coursed random rubble-stone, is set in parkland and can be reached only by the footpath behind the manor. Within, a low pointed arch with scalloped capitals separates the chancel from the nave. The wagon roof is modern and the walls have been skinned, but the stone is of good quality. The church is beautifully cared for; its small size must encourage those tireless volunteers with polish and brush, but it is remarkable, as so often in the Cotswolds, that as numbers in the congregation allegedly decline, the commitment to making the church look attractive seems to increase. Is this the law of diminishing returns, or parishioners who perhaps love churches more than Church?

Daglingworth

GLOUCESTERSHIRE
OS 163 993050
3 miles north-west of Cirencester

THE VILLAGE IS IN A BEAUTIFUL VALLEY, a tributary of the River Churn which it joins at Cirencester. It is a remote and lovely spot, famous for its Saxon church, dedicated to the Holy Rood (**91**). This was much restored between 1845 and 1850, but the nave roof, its south wall and the porch survived, together with the tower, a sturdy Perpendicular construction with diagonal buttresses but, as so often in Gloucestershire, without pinnacles. At nearly all its angles the church has long-and-short-work – stones placed with their long sides alternately upright and horizontal, the Saxon method of making quoins – and it is for its Saxon survivals that this church is most renowned. The south doorway and the sundial above are both Saxon, although the porch, and the door itself with its fine woodwork, date from the fifteenth century. On the east gable, at the end of the chancel, high up, is a tiny Saxon crucifix.

Inside are three sculptures dating from about 1050, discovered during the nineteenth-century restoration. The Crucifixion, set in the chancel arch, is the most important. Christ, his head, hair and

loin-cloth especially well preserved, is flanked by the soldiers Longinus and Stephaton, who bear the emblems of the Crucifixion: to the left the spear and scourge, to the right the reed and sponge. They are a little damaged, and the top left-hand corner is missing altogether. To the keen and critical eye these sculptures are doubtless a little unyielding and lacking in sensitivity, yet their simplicity carries strong conviction and their solemnity is deeply moving. The other panels, in the north aisle, are single figures: St Peter with an over-large key to the heavenly gates (no question here of who is keeper of the Kingdom) and Christ enthroned. These carvings look as if they may be by the same hand, crude but vigorous.

In the village are two dovecots. One is in the grounds of the former rectory, and both buildings date from shortly after the restoration of the church. The other, at the manor house, three or four centuries older than most buildings of this type, is medieval and therefore quite a rarity. It is circular and still preserves its 'potence' (from the French meaning 'gallows'), a horizontal beam

Saxon sculpture, Holy Rood, Daglingworth
◁ Saxon sculpture, Holy Rood, Daglingworth
◁◁ Long-and-short work, Holy Rood, Daglingworth
Holy Rood and the Rectory, ▷ Daglingworth

stemming from a central pivot on the end of which was mounted a ladder to enable the keeper to move freely round the nests. There are cottages and barns all in the ownership of the Duchy of Cornwall either side of the stream, a village hall, and a number of other pleasant houses. Daglingworth House, square and no-nonsense Georgian, close by the church, is the most substantial. The oolitic limestone is much in evidence, the right material in the right place.

Didmarton

GLOUCESTERSHIRE
OS 173 823874
7 miles south-west of Tetbury

THE VILLAGE HAS THE MISFORTUNE to be on the main road, but there are some inviting inns and houses; an octagonal gazebo announces Kingsmead House, and the centre of Didmarton Manor survives, clipped of its wings in the eighteenth century when it became the rectory of the neighbouring parish church of St Lawrence. The medieval church is now luckily in the care of the Redundant Churches Fund, under whose auspices it was rescued from dereliction and then delicately restored. It became redundant as early as 1872, when it was decided to build anew rather than restore. The result was on one hand T. H. Wyatt's rather ordinary church of St Michael, which contains some resited monuments, presumably from the old church; and on the other hand St Lawrence, a precious survivor, but only just.

St Lawrence has a near-perfect eighteenth-century interior with box pews, a splendid three-decker pulpit set between two windows within a single gently curving arch carried on pilasters, and behind the altar a decalogue, retrieved from a nearby farmyard. The colour scheme is a pale green, handsome and assured. From an earlier medieval church have come a piscina and a Norman font, now with an eighteenth-century wooden cover. For this interior we should be doubly grateful: to the Victorians who left well alone, and to the Redundant Churches Fund which at the eleventh hour responded with such sensitivity to the challenge of our own day.

Dodington

GLOUCESTERSHIRE
OS 172 755798
3½ miles south-east of Chipping Sodbury

THE HOUSE AND PARK are not at the moment open to the public. Bath Lodge, James Wyatt's rotunda (**93**) set beside the A46 north of exit 18 on the M4, beckons somewhat frustratingly. It is approached through huge gate-piers, heavily rusticated and with niches. It is a splendid creation in ashlar, patchy in places and in need of repair, and with a dome, capped in lead, which rises above a Tuscan colonnade. It is an appetizer that will one day, let us hope, again be a prelude to the main course. Dodington Park is one of Gloucestershire's largest stately homes. It is a rebuilding of 1798 –1813 by Wyatt of an earlier gabled house of the Tudor period, surrounded by a park where Capability Brown had already worked his genius on the landscape. He provided two lakes and a cascade, opened up new vistas, and made a setting of sophistication and delight in a valley of wooded hills. It is the art that conceals art.

The church of St Mary is adjacent to the house and stands on the

Bath Lodge rotunda,
Dodington Park

site of a medieval church, completely rebuilt by Wyatt at the time
the house was under construction. It is in the unusual form of a
Greek cross, surmounted by a dome resting on Doric columns of
elegant proportions, and is directly connected at the south to the
house. It is little used and in need of a complete and careful
restoration to reveal its full potential. In this setting, and as part of
the ensemble, it is vital that this should be achieved.

DOWDESWELL, just south of the A40 trunk road as it descends
past a reservoir on its way to Cheltenham, has quite a lot to show,
but interest focuses on the setting and the church of St Michael.
The latter is strikingly situated on a steep slope; to the east are trees.
Below is a splendid group of farm buildings which includes not
only an eight-gabled sixteenth-century house, but outhouses, barn,
cowshed and a dovecot built over an arch with gable-ends and a
lantern (**95**). All of the buildings, it would appear, are of the same
period. There is a spectacular view beyond.

The church is cruciform, mainly of the fourteenth century and of
ashlar throughout, although the roofs have dull machine-made

Dowdeswell

GLOUCESTERSHIRE
OS 163 002199
4½ miles south-east of Cheltenham

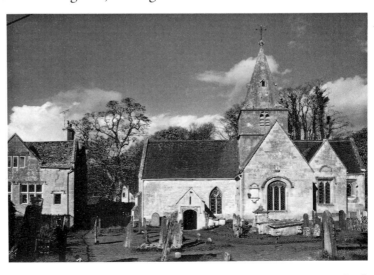

St Michael, Dowdeswell

tiles – fortunately Staffordshire blue rather than pink. There is a small central tower and stone spire of 1577, and a tympanum of Norman origin from an earlier building. It depicts the Tree of Life and has been set into the gable of a nineteenth-century organ chamber. Inside are two galleries, one at the west end which belonged to the manor and another at the north for the rectory, both reached only by private exterior access. There are some fine monuments, especially the bust of William Rogers (1734) on the north wall of the chancel, set between columns supporting a pediment and adorned with cherubs and swags of flowers. The tablets to members of the Rich and Rogers families are also of good quality, and in the chancel is the brass (*c.*1520) of a priest clad in a gorgeous processional cope.

There is a fair sprinkling of substantial houses in the parish. Dowdeswell Court is south of the church, built *c.*1834 in ashlar in the Corinthian style. It has lost its top storey. The former Rectory and Upper Dowdeswell Manor House are a little further away, both early houses which have been spruced up over the centuries. The Manor has a touch of the baroque over the front door and two gate-posts with ornate urns. The Rectory gained a Doric portico when a new front was added in the 1780s; they need scarcely have bothered, for the most virulently hirsute creeper in the Cotswolds obscures all.

Duntisbourne Rouse

GLOUCESTERSHIRE
OS 163 985060
4 miles north-west of Cirencester

THIS IS ONE OF FOUR DUNTISBOURNES (frequently pronounced Dunsbourne) that inhabit the idyllic valley of the Dun, not much more than a stream which flows into the River Churn at Cirencester. The village is enchanting. The tiny church of St Michael stands on the side of a steep hill, and is approached by a straight, gently sloping grass path to which, by the happiest of chances, the church is not end-on but at a slight angle (**98**). Everything is in miniature. At first not much is to be seen but the tiny saddle-backed tower, Perpendicular with an Elizabethan upper stage. The masonry of this little church is appropriately rough, but it has a lovely stone-slated roof. Within, simplicity matches the mood. The nave is Saxon, the chancel Norman, and the box pews and panelling, separated though they are from the structure by five centuries or more, seem to suit so well. There are some late medieval stalls with misericords, tip-up seats carved with male heads (or are they lions?) flanked by vine leaves. All five are nearly identical, which is unusual. The site is so steep that it was possible to underpin the chancel with a minute crypt, empty and disused now, but with its own unglazed east window. Everything here is diminutive except one's pleasure; if ever a church was marked A for atmosphere, this is it.

Duntisbourne Rouse is the most rewarding of these little villages, but the valley is well worth at least half a day. At Middle Duntisbourne, half a mile to the north, there is a ford across the

Dun, with cottages either side, a scene of unspoiled charm. At Duntisbourne Leer, which takes its name from the abbey of Lire in Normandy, in whose possession the manor was until 1416, there is another ford, a cottage with pigeon-holes and two attractive old farmhouses, one with a brewhouse attached. Duntisbourne Leer is no more than a hamlet of Duntisbourne Abbots, once in the possession of Gloucester Abbey. It is the most substantial of these settlements, rising above another ford, where the stream of the Dun was diverted at one point to clean cart-wheels and horses' feet. The village, a delicious array of ashlar, rubblestone and stone tiles, clusters around the parish church of St Peter. This is much altered within and undistinguished, save for some medieval ironwork on the south door.

About a mile to the south is Pinbury Park. This is a medieval building in origin, and once belonged to the nuns of Caen, but it was converted in the seventeenth century and became the home of the county historian, Sir Robert Atkyns, who died in 1711. His *Ancient and Present State of Gloucestershire*, a classic among county histories, with engravings of the major houses, was reprinted in facsimile in the 1970s. The house was again sensitively reworked by the Barnsley brothers, Ernest and Sydney, along with Ernest Gimson, who also lived here at the turn of the century. The setting is superb above the Gloucestershire beech-woods and the 'Golden Valley' of the River Frome.

Dursley

GLOUCESTERSHIRE
OS 162 758979
4 miles north of Wotton-under-Edge

DURSLEY was an important medieval wool town and more recently an industrial centre for the making of cloth. The local stone, something of a speciality, is a tufa, of geologically recent age, formed by spring water bubbling from more ancient limestones; the water is impregnated with calcium carbonate which hardens and accumulates on exposure to the air. This process gives the stone its pitted appearance, rather like a petrified sponge, and the quarry which was at the lower end of the town was worked until the present century.

The greyish stone is much in evidence in the parish church of St James, not only in the older parts of the medieval building, but also in the restoration by Sir Thomas Jackson in the late 1860s. There is a good sponge-like example inside on the easternmost arch of the north arcade, and another at the base of the east arch of the south arcade. This interior is spacious and light, and the east window, an Ascension by Burlison and Grylls, put in about the time of Jackson's restoration, is of high quality, rich in colour, and far superior to the rest of the glass in the church. The roof was raised in the restoration to accommodate a clerestory, but the main beams and angels of the kingposts look original.

The surprise is the tower, built 1707–9 to replace the spire and part of the medieval tower which had fallen in 1698. The design is by Thomas Sumsion of Colerne, 'one of the last master masons',

St James, Dursley ▷

[98]   St Michael, Duntisbourne Rouse, Gloucestershire

Market Place and Long Street,
Dursley

H. M. Colvin* explains, 'to carry on authentic medieval traditions
of design into the early eighteenth century, the members of
[whose] family continued to follow the mason's trade in Colerne
until the war of 1939–45'. His tower of three stages was based on
the one in his own village in Wiltshire, with diagonal buttresses and
with the addition of a fine crown (**99**), sporting battlements and
pinnacles in the style of Gloucester Cathedral.

Parts of the town have been somewhat spoilt, and its old mills are
now inhabited by some unsightly modern light industry. But the
town centre has much good building such as Lloyds Bank in Long
Street, early eighteenth-century, asymmetrical with four bays and
occupying a site near the Market House of 1738, which incorporates the Town Hall and boasts a statue of Queen Anne (**101**). The
roughcast does not quite achieve the dignity to which the building
aspires. It is well worth walking the length of Long Street, resisting
the temptations of the Old Bell Hotel, down to the bottom of the
hill, where the Priory, a clothier's house of the mid-sixteenth
century, its rubblestone albeit all painted, ends a wholly satisfying
sequence of town architecture.

Dyrham

AVON (*formerly* GLOUCESTERSHIRE)
OS 172 743758
5½ miles south-east of Chipping
Sodbury

DYRHAM IS APPROACHED through a pair of lodges on the A46
Bath road, along a drive which curls its way down through what
has been a park for fallow deer for over 1,000 years. The setting in a
hollow under the escarpment is perfect, certainly if you are first to
arrive, for the rows of parked cars that assemble during visiting
days in front of the east elevation are a sad blot on this delectable
landscape. The park was once a tremendous formal garden, laid out
at the end of the seventeenth century by George London, one of the
most famous gardeners of his time, with terraces, fountains, a

* *A Biographical Dictionary of British Architects 1600–1840*, John Murray, 1978.

Town Hall, Dursley

Dyrham Park

cascade and a canal. Only the statue of Neptune on the hill survives as testimony to the grandeur displayed in the much reproduced Kips engraving of 1712. These gardens must have been a magnificent sight.

The builder of Dyrham was William Blathwayt, whose family lived in the house until the 1950s when it passed to the care of the National Trust. Blathwayt was an adept servant of the Crown; he had met the varying demands of Charles II and James II and at the time of the Glorious Revolution of 1688 was Secretary for War, and a firm supporter of William of Orange. His interiors reflect, understandably and perhaps diplomatically, a passion for all things Dutch. He married well. Mary Wynter brought house and fortune with her.

Blathwayt started rebuilding the old Tudor house on the west side where a little-known French architect, Hauduroy*, provided him in 1692 with two storeys, small, manageable and unpretentious, with a terrace overlooking extensive lawns, reached by a double flight of steps (**102**). Ten years later, he was able to employ a court architect and assistant of Wren, William Talman, who had worked at Chatsworth. Talman's east front, which has the entrance, is a much grander affair, but still domestic, and owes more to Wren than to the style of Vanbrugh or Hawksmoor. It is thirteen bays wide and three storeys high, with a doorway of Tuscan columns but no pediment, and a balustrade above a bold cornice, on which perches a huge eagle carved by John Harvey of Bath. An orangery, set with massive Tuscan columns in the style of Versailles, is adjacent to the south, and is matched by a lower extension to the north, which runs out of space and appears to bump rather abruptly into the hillside.

The pale-yellow oolite, worked by the local masons Philip West from Corsham and Richard Broad of Box, came mostly from the quarry at Tolldown, one and a half miles to the north-east. The stables, a long range facing west with a cupola too small for comfort, were built 1698–9, also to a design by Talman, and have mullioned and transomed windows. The original sash-framed windows of the 1692 house, some of which survive, had small lights – eight up and four across, thirty-two to the window – but most were replaced in the mid- or later eighteenth century by the elegant thin glazing bars to be seen today.

Talman's house, put back to back with Hauduroy's with a Great Hall and Dining-Room wedged between them, makes for something of an odd plan: the lofty Hall looks down a sort of architectural corridor between high blocks, while the Dining-Room looks directly on to a steep bank. The other rooms are not large, but there is fine furniture, including the state bed that Blathwayt kept prepared for Queen Anne, and a lot of Delftware and minor Dutch

* Perhaps Samuel Hauduroy. For more detail *see* article by Mark Girouard, *Country Life* (15 Feb. 1962).

paintings. The staircase of Virginian walnut painted white is the work of Robert Barker. The interior is enjoyable but not greatly distinguished; the mansion stately but no masterpiece.

The church of St Peter is approached by a gap in a magnificent high hedge on the west side of the house. It is charming, and the stonework excellent. Within, the Jacobean pulpit, the brass of 1416 and four little figures of fifteenth-century glass in the east window are all worthy of note, but pride of place goes to a wall monument near the private entrance to the house in the south aisle. It is dated 1710 and carved by John Harvey, in memory of Mary Blathwayt (*née* Wynter) and her parents John and Frances, whose fortune helped make the recreation of Dyrham possible.

Eastleach Turville
GLOUCESTERSHIRE
OS 163 203053
5 miles north of Lechlade

Centaur corbel, St John,
Elkstone ▷

Tympanum, St John,
Elkstone ▷

THIS IS A ROMANTIC SPOT: a heavenly setting, and not just one, but two medieval churches, separated by a mere stone's throw beside the rippling waters of the River Leach. The river is crossed by a road-bridge and a foot-bridge of large flat paving-stones, called Keble's bridge, after the family who held the manor here in the fifteenth century. Their distinguished descendant John, author of *The Christian Year*, became non-resident curate in 1815. The church south of the stream is dedicated to St Michael and St Martin. St Martin gives the hamlet its name, although more frequently it is referred to as Bouthrop.

St Michael and St Martin* is the humbler of the two churches, roughcast, with a rather squat tower, but with three attractive Decorated windows in the north transept. Within it is virtually unspoiled, with oil lamps, seventeenth-century pews, and some medieval oak benches. Nothing could be more rural. St Andrew is transitional and Early English, a charming little church set in a well-kept churchyard with some eighteenth-century tombstones, mostly now against the church wall. It has a saddleback tower, and a south porch with a Norman doorway and tympanum of Christ in Majesty with angels, now much worn. Three lancets at the east end are set in a deeply moulded triplet of arches.

A wooded slope provides the backdrop for St Michael and St Martin; the village rises on the bank opposite behind St Andrew. There are a number of substantial houses, notably Greenbury House, dated 1738 but with a Gothick addition and a bay window overlooking the valley. Round the corner to the west are two parallel streets, one higher than the other, with cottages, some old, but mostly built in the last century for the workers on Sir Thomas Bazley's estate at Hatherop. The two churches in such proximity are explained, it seems, by two hamlets originally separate and in the hands of different manorial lords; the piety which built a church for each community has helped to create one of the most memorable scenes in the Cotswolds.

* Now in the care of the Redundant Churches Fund.

Elkstone

A SIZEABLE DEVELOPMENT and conversion of farm buildings just south of the church is nearing completion. It is an expensive, well-crafted operation which uses stone cladding to conceal the inevitable breeze blocks. Its good-neighbourliness is gratifying, although it will change the character and scale of the village. Nothing much need detain us here, save the old Georgian rectory and its Victorian replacement, but the little church is an experience never forgotten. St John, Elkstone, is the finest Norman church in the Cotswolds, an area rich by any standards in the Romanesque.

The original tower which divided the chancel from the nave collapsed, and was replaced about 1370 at the west. This is plain and lacks pinnacles but a lot is going on up there – shawm, citole, and a cacophony of grotesques. The carving continues to north and south on an extremely well-preserved corbel table, contemporary with the early church which is almost wholly *c*.1160. Here is a fantastic ribald crew; a centaur, a griffin, a snake-like creature, a ram, an elephant who may never forget but seems to have lost half his trunk, a devil with horns, and many more.

All this is merely by way of *hors d'oeuvres*. The south door, protected by a porch, has a tympanum, artistically crude perhaps for some tastes, but extraordinary in its impact. A Christ in Majesty with the hand of God above is surrounded by the emblems of the Evangelists with the Lamb of God in place of St Matthew's winged man; there is a dove to the right and a seraph to the left. Long beakheads – half-human, half-birdlike creatures – abound, and

Chancel, St John,
Elkstone

deeply cut chevrons decorate the orders of the arch. Familiar grotesques, carved perhaps by the same hand as at the corbel table, have found a home in the capitals and columns flanking the jambs of the door.

Within, under an arch-braced roof with collars and wind-braces, the church divides neatly into four, tower, nave, choir and sanctuary. Two low arches at the chancel immediately catch the eye. They are both richly adorned with chevron, and at the end of the arch between nave and choir, large heads, alligator- or dragon-like, appear. The positioning of these rebuilt arches is a legacy from the original tower which rose above, but its effect is to create an almost tunnel-like perspective to the tiny sanctuary beyond. This has a ribbed vault, and an east window, again profusely decorated, lit by modern glass designed by Henry Payne of Stroud in 1929. Some Victorian glass was removed within memory from the west window and south chancel. Its replacement in 1959 by W. T. Carter Shapland, while doubtless an improvement, still does not quite befit its surroundings.

Columbarium, St John,
Elkstone

In the nave there is a Perpendicular font (the familiar octagonal Gloucestershire design), a Jacobean pulpit, and a made-up reading-desk, taken from the tester of the pulpit and dated 1604. After the drama of the Romanesque, a narrow spiral stairway behind the pulpit invites us to investigate above. It leads, indeed, to further adventure, to a columbarium or dovecot. It fills a space created when the chancel roof was raised to the height of the nave after the fall of the Norman tower. There are many nesting openings in the walls, and at the east, a small lancet window where the birds flew in and out. Could any dove wish for a holier habitation?

Fairford

GLOUCESTERSHIRE
OS 163 152012
10 miles east of Cirencester

MANY VISITORS TO FAIRFORD leave too little time for the town, for they come first to see the celebrated church, and that can leave even the most untiring amateur of churches exhausted. The town lies on the River Coln, five miles to the west of Lechlade where it joins the upper reaches of the Thames. To the south, Fairford has an aerodrome, once the noisy home of Brabazon and then Concorde, and still operational. This notwithstanding, the town is a pleasant place, stone-built throughout, but on a busy main road. It has one wide space, inevitably disfigured with parking, which provides access to Fairford Park, where a modern school now occupies the site of a sizeable mansion demolished in the 1950s. There are a number of eighteenth-century buildings well worth a glance: Fairford House, with its hipped stone roof, Colstone House (perhaps the best in the town), ashlar with pediment and cornice, and a rusticated ground floor giving strength and dignity to its appearance, and adjacent to the churchyard a school built in 1738, still with casement windows when sashes had become the fashion. For the High Church party, a pilgrimage to John Keble's birthplace along the London Road to the east is obligatory; in the other direction pursuers of the picturesque will promenade to the Mill, prettily sited where the canal of the Park once more resumes its role as the River Coln (**2/3, 110**).

St Mary, Fairford

The church of St Mary is of considerable importance. Apart from the lower end of the central tower, which dates from the early fifteenth century, the whole church was rebuilt between 1490 and 1500 by John Tame, a rich wool merchant. It is therefore an exceptionally homogeneous example of the late high Perpendicular. The stone is a yellowish ashlar, in places paling to buff. What is immediately and strikingly apparent is the size of the windows and of the numerous crocketed pinnacles above. This is a sumptuous exterior. At both levels, above the clerestories and above the aisles, the walls have solid parapets, and on the string courses just below is a whole host of carved figures, many of which are grotesque animals copied from old bestiaries. These figures are most spirited, and one in particular, on the south side, is masterly: often identified as a jester in large head-dress (109), he dangles a leg as if to jump. For the more scatologically inclined who view this jester from a few paces to the west, this interpretation is too fastidious by half.

The south porch has a fan-vault, but the tower is not of the first rank. It does not soar sufficiently, and has too many contrived rectangular motifs; and at the top, the corners of the pierced parapet are sliced off to accommodate coupled pinnacles. It has a congregation of grotesques which include a huge head of a man, a hand holding a scourge, and a griffin. Armorial bearings are in evidence too: John Tame's own, a wyvern in combat with a lion,

Parapet sculpture, St Mary,
Fairford

and the arms and badge of Warwick, a muzzled bear climbing a ragged staff. The earls of Warwick held the manor in the Middle Ages. Local trades get a look-in, too: blacksmith's pincers, the hunter's horn, horseshoes, and a wine vat. On the west face is a portrayal of Christ wearing the crown of thorns, primitive but decidedly effective. The churchyard has Georgian gravestones and table tombs, but is too cluttered, and the quality of the funereal furniture is uneven.

Inside there is plenty of light. The nave has elegant and unusual piers composed of sixteen colonnettes, groups of three at each of the cardinal points of the compass with one in each of the diagonals. On one of the tower arches can be seen the remains of wall paintings; one angel, high up on the west wall, is well preserved, and a St Christopher looks down from the north wall of the nave aisle. Wooden screens are something of a rarity in Gloucestershire, and their presence here, almost complete with choir-screen and parclose, is of considerable interest even if they are artistically run-of-the-mill. In the choir are well-preserved misericords, a little dark and over-varnished, but with lively, familiar subjects – harvest, fox and geese, the drunken husband – and one portrait with a huge head which particularly haunts the memory. Nearby are the fine sixteenth-century brasses of the Tame family, father and son and their wives.

Everyone who visits Fairford comes to see the stained glass (**111**); it dates from about 1490–1520 and is justifiably famous in that it all came from the same workshop, probably that of Henry VII's master glass-painter Barnard Flower, who employed English craftsman as well as perhaps Flemish and French. The sequence portrays the whole Catholic faith starting with the Fall, depicted on the north side by the Lady Chapel, and proceeding clockwise by way of Christ's Birth, Crucifixion and Resurrection to the Last Judgement in the great window at the west. The scheme is based on an early printed book, illustrated with woodcuts, the *Biblia Pauperum*, and is lucidly described in David Verey's Pevsner volume* and in various useful booklets and guides generally available for sale in the church.

There are twenty-eight windows, including eight in the nave clerestory. They repay careful study, but are something of a disappointment. The colours lack radiance; the glass is more white than anything else, and the colour is of limited range, consisting mainly of grey-blue, ruby and yellow. The single figures in the nave clerestory, prophets, apostles and evangelists, are mostly in sound condition, as is most of the window in the Chapel of the Holy Sacrament which depicts the Transfiguration and two of Christ's appearances after the Resurrection. The east window, recounting the Passion and the events of Holy Week, is in good repair, but much of the other narrative glass is less so, and the top half of the

* *Gloucestershire: The Cotswolds*, second edition, Penguin Books, 1979.

Fairford Park, Gloucestershire

Last Judgement was entirely renewed, rather strikingly, by Hardman of Birmingham in the nineteenth century.

The Fairford glass is interesting rather than thrilling; it lacks the lustre and sparkle which is the special attribute of the best late Gothic examples. None the less, this is the only parish church in England fortunate enough to have retained a complete set of pre-Reformation windows.

Fifteenth-century
stained glass,
Fairford

Farnborough

WARWICKSHIRE
OS 151 434495
5½ miles north of Banbury

OLD COTTAGES AND HOUSES in the attractive local Hornton stone cluster round the gates of the Hall, which dominates the village. Even the church of St Botolph is little more than a side-show of the estate. There is not much of interest here, save the Norman survivals at the south door and in the chancel arch, and the monument to Mrs Wagstaffe, 1667, decoratively set with a long and affecting brass inscription to 'a saint on earth'. The east window of 1856, by Wailes, is a brute.

For nearly three centuries the Hall was in the ownership of the Holbech family (pronounced 'holbeech') before it passed to the National Trust in 1960. It is set in a silvan landscape and surrounded by a deer park, lawns and water. A huge cedar of Lebanon takes pride of place and a spectacular mown terrace rises gently from the back of the house past a temple and an oval pavilion to a distant obelisk. There are views across to Warmington and Edge Hill, a panorama under threat by the projected route of the M40. The earliest part of the house dates from 1684 and is at the west front. This is of seven bays with balustrade, but feels altogether too cramped with its central doorway only just fitting its allotted space and an awkward little dormer above. There are two stylish rainwater heads in lead, but the glazing bars on the front are a little thin, and must have been inserted a century after the house was built.

The north side, of 1750, has five bays flanked by projecting wings. Like the south side, of about the same date, it is more assured and more sophisticated. Some of the thicker glazing bars are original. The entrance hall has a rococo ceiling by William Perritt, a plasterer born in Yorkshire, and his ceiling pattern is repeated exactly on the floor in dark and light stone. There is a fine chimney-piece with a leaf frieze supported by paunchy corbels. Busts of emperors in oval recesses gaze out from just below the ceiling, seeming to seek the warmth of the fire. The staircase, partly renewed, is set in an oblong well; it is simple but of satisfying proportions, wide and shallow treads only five inches high. The plaster decoration is lavish, with wreaths of flowers under an oval skylight dome of *c*.1690, and panels, later in date, but still effective.

The Dining-Room is the *pièce de résistance*. The stucco is profuse, with flowers and medallions at the ceiling, and the walls pure rococo, with trophies of emperors and musical instruments in abundance, bows and arrows and guns, significant perhaps of a less agreeable aspect of Holbech country life. The white marble chimney-piece is only a little more restrained. At the overmantel and to either side the stucco was designed to frame paintings by Canaletto and Pannini, sold as long ago as 1929, and now replaced by copies. The oval mirror between the windows has a cornucopia of flowers and fruit, without symmetry and all of a flourish. The mahogany doors, handsomely waxed and polished, with original brass lock-plates and handles, stand sentinel in wonder.

FILKINS, and the equally unusually named Broughton Poggs, the Broughton of the Poggs (as in Stoke Poges), are almost contiguous villages on the western edge of the county. St Peter, Filkins, is a mid-nineteenth-century building by G. E. Street with a steep pitch to its roof. It is in the French Gothic style, with an apse decorated in gold-blue stars on a blue ground, and, for its period and its architect, is happily reticent and welcome. Outside, the semicircular apse subtly becomes a hexagon at window level.

The village has some substantial houses and picturesque cottages, mostly of the seventeenth century, and some notable examples of limestone slab fencing, much older than many of the houses. These slabs measure three feet by two or more and mark a boundary with some determination; stone here must be plentiful indeed to allow such extravagance. In 1981 a small quarry was opened in the village for the production of limestone roofing slates, 'presents' as they are uniquely called in the Cotswolds, once in plentiful supply from Naunton and elsewhere in the locality. The stone is found near the surface or in shallow pits and is naturally fissile. It splits while still in the ground, and produces slates almost ready-made, except for holing and shaping – presents indeed for those who work them. Filkins has a number of houses roofed with these slates including some north-east of the church, which were built by the local authority in the 1950s in the local hard rubble-stone. They suit the locality admirably.

BADMINTON MEANS SHUTTLECOCKS, horse trials, the Beaufort Hunt, and the grandest mansion in the Cotswolds. The village is approached along a wide street bordered by estate cottages, then by a discreet Victorian range which houses an even more discreet post office, and finally by almshouses, with the ducal coat of arms in the pediment. It is all very feudal, and beautifully kept. Every building is stone, often roughcast, and sometimes with a yellow ochre colour-wash, an attractive estate livery.

The great house, which is not regularly open to the public, dates from the 1690s. It is set in an immense park. The architect is undocumented, although many famous names have contributed to its development. The house was enlarged c.1740 with wings to the east and west, and a pavilion to the south to make for symmetry on that side. The north front, the central bay of which has bold rustication, is on a majestic scale, and even the twin cupolas, designed by Kent and made of wood, are rendered to simulate stone. This is undeniably a mansion fit for a grandee, but architecturally it is rather a jumble.

The Hall, where the game of badminton originated, has magnificent decoration, probably the work of Kent. The Dining-Room has a Grinling Gibbons chimney-piece in limewood, wondrously carved with fruit, fish and birds; it dates from 1683. The Library was Gothicized by Wyatville in 1811. From here a corridor leads to the church, or more specifically to the Somerset family pew, furnished with fireplace and easy chairs.

The church, dedicated to St Michael, replaced a medieval one which was sited further to the west and demolished by the fifth duke. The architect was Charles Evans, a carpenter by trade, who provided a plain classical exterior, and an interior derivative of Gibbs' St Martin-in-the-Fields. The church is spacious and unexciting, but there are two grand monuments. That of the first duke of Beaufort, who died in 1699, was brought here from St George's Chapel in Windsor in 1875, when the chancel and apse were added. It is by Grinling Gibbons and conceived on a prodigious scale with Corinthian columns rising to a cornice over twenty feet from the ground, where a cushion supports the duke's coronet. Gibbons's carving is superb, but being in stone it lacks the delicacy of his work in wood. The second and third dukes are commemorated by Rysbrack in a fine monument, signed and dated 1754. They are depicted resplendent in Roman costume, with drapery tumbling down over an elaborate coffin. Rysbrack was also responsible for the monument to the fourth duke; the fifth in line had to make do with Westmacott, as did the fourth duke's wife.

Capability Brown laid out the park. It was William Kent who provided its most original and extraordinary ornament, the Palladian Worcester Lodge, two and a half miles to the north, at the end of the three-mile ride and precisely in line with the north entrance of the mansion. Park buildings and follies abound – a ragged castle, lodges and a castle barn – but Worcester Lodge is something special. It is, in effect, a dining-room over an archway. Dating from 1746, it is rusticated at the ground floor, but built of a superb ashlar tinged with pink at the upper storey, with a pediment containing the ducal arms, and topped out by an octagonal saucer-dome in lead. The proportions are perhaps not quite correct; the first storey could be just a little more generous in height, and the dome a trifle less heavy, but the craftsmanship is admirable.

Sacheverell Sitwell* was rhapsodic in his admiration for this building, but it must be pure romance to suggest, as he did, that the view at supper on a summer evening could ever extend to the Bristol Channel and across to the Welsh hills. A twilight haze can certainly be deceptive, but so can a good port.

The Guitings
GLOUCESTERSHIRE
OS 163 092279
8 miles west of Stow-on-the-Wold

GUITING IS DERIVATIVE of the old English word *gyte*, meaning a flood or torrent, and it seems to have been the old name of the Upper Windrush. Two villages take their name from it: **Guiting Power** at the confluence of two streams that marks the beginning of the Windrush proper (OS 163 099249), and **Temple Guiting** two miles upstream. Guiting Power is a sizeable and attractive village, spread out round a large green, with a Norman church somewhat hidden under later alterations and a fairly severe

* *British Architects and Craftsmen*, Batsford, 1945.

restoration at the turn of this century. It is almost a Greek cross in plan, with a squat embattled tower at the west. The famous Guiting quarries are not far to the north, so it is not surprising that all the houses, including those built by the local authority, are of stone. Only the occasional concrete tiled roofs intrude.

Temple Guiting House and the church, shyly revealing themselves from a setting of wood and parkland on the approach from the south, are an enchanting sight. The church of St Mary is architecturally a mixture. The large tower is clumsy but redeemed by a charming clock of 1870. Inside there are three windows of sixteenth-century glass with tall figures of considerable dignity, perhaps of Flemish or German origin, remarkably complete and well preserved. Each figure is about two feet high: the Virgin Mary, St James the Less, and Mary Magdalene, the most 'Renaissance' of the group. The colours are off-white, blue, ruby, yellow and a little green. Above the tower arch is a specially fine royal arms of George II in white plaster. The Georgian pulpit is of oak, inlaid and richly carved, and to the north is a pretty wall monument to John Beale, 1774, with two putti and an angel riding on what looks like a sea-monster. An uncompromising 'cyclopean' eye glowers from below.

Outside, at the east end of the nave on the south side, is a little lancet window with ballflower, the dripstone of which ends in jesters' heads, a rare miniature. The north end of the north transept has a Venetian window. Naturally enough the church is built of local stone, too yellow sometimes for comfort, but luckily it has plenty of lichen, red, brown and grey, to soften the effect. Temple Guiting House is Georgian and ashlared; Manor Farm opposite is Tudor, long, low and picturesque. They contrast effectively and make a captivating group.

Fifteenth-century stained glass, Hailes

Hailes

GLOUCESTERSHIRE
OS 150 050300
3 miles north-east of Winchcombe

> By goddes precious herte, and by his nayles
> And the blode of Christ that is in Hayles
> Seven is my chaunce, and thyn is cink and treye . . .

THUS THE PARDONER on the pain of idle swearing in Chaucer's *Canterbury Tales*; just over 100 years earlier, in 1270, Edmund, a nephew of Henry III and son of the abbey's founder, had presented to this great Cistercian foundation a relic of the Holy Blood, guaranteed as genuine by no less than the pope himself. It was to be denounced at the time of the Dissolution as 'but honey clarified and coloured with saffron'.

By the custody of this relic, the abbey achieved great fame and became the goal of national and even international pilgrimage. It became extremely wealthy in land and gifts offered by countless pilgrims. The relic was enshrined in a rebuilding of the east end of the church, in a chevet, or apse with an ambulatory of radiating chapels, as in the abbeys at Westminster or Tewkesbury. Little of the abbey remains apart from some miscellaneous arches, once part of a large cloister: a poignant monument to an age of faith, whatever one thinks of relics and church wealth. After the Dissolution, the stone (the local oolite, with a blue lias for the details) was pillaged and travelled far and wide, and parts of the ambulatory turned up in the tower arch and west window at Teddington, eight miles to the west. Cypresses once marked the site of the piers of the church, but they became too big and had to be removed. The museum contains a collection of floor tiles and a series of huge bosses from the chapter house, the largest of which must weigh a ton or more. They are mostly carved with elaborate conventional foliage. There is also an excellent exhibition of the mason's craft in the museum garden. It shows examples of carved details, well labelled, set in context, and cross-referenced with other contemporary church-building.

The abbey enjoys a romantic setting amongst trees and wooded hills, watered by the brook of the infant River Isbourne which flows north to join the Avon at Evesham. Appropriately enough, it was founded (in 1246) in romantic circumstances – as a result of a vow made by Richard, earl of Cornwall, after his escape from shipwreck off the Scillies. It was colonized from Beaulieu, which had been founded by Richard's father, King John.

The parish church, whose dedication is not known, predates the monastery (which subsequently took it into ownership) by about 100 years. It is chiefly of the fourteenth century, with an aisleless nave and chancel under a slate roof. The walls are of a yellow-golden rubblestone, perhaps from Guiting, two miles to the east. The church has no tower, but a quaint bellcote at the west, partly timbered. Inside it is cold and damp, but an appealing little church all the same, with stone flags for the floor and rough village pews dating from before the Reformation. The chancel has a plastered wagon-roof with some timbers revealed. The screen appears to be of the same period; rustic and with no loft. In the chancel there are many tiles brought from the abbey opposite, and some pretty fifteenth-century glass in the east window depicting the Apostles, removed from the abbey church and only installed here in 1903 (**115**).

There are also wall paintings, well preserved and well restored. In the chancel they depict fantastic monsters like the griffin, with the head and wings of an eagle but the body of a lion, and the heraldic devices of the abbey's founder and his wife. Either side of the east window are censing angels, and on the north wall St Catherine and St Margaret. In the nave, the paintings were only uncovered as recently as 1970. To the north is St Christopher and to the south a hunting scene, with three lithe and lively hounds about to devour a terrified hare.

The church has been well served by the deft touch of its restorers. The furnishings remain almost intact: pulpit, panelling, choir-stalls and altar are all from the seventeenth century, and there is a box pew with some original ironwork. The last restoration was in 1961; how sensible it is, as far as possible, to leave well alone.

THE VILLAGE has some attractive old cottages and barns, sandwiched between the former main road and the Northleach bypass to the north. From the churchyard, early in the morning and late in the evening (for it shows its north face), there is a fine view of Northleach tower. The church of St George is Norman from the outside but almost wholly Victorian within. The Norman arrangement of three sections survives, with a nave and chancel divided by what was probably a small central tower; the east end, in its pristine state, would be an excellent example of Norman architecture on a small scale, with carvings of doves neck-to-neck drinking from a bowl on the capitals of the sanctuary arch. The vault is similar to that at St John, Elkstone. In 1871, however, only three years after a heavy restoration by G. E. Street, the Revd W. Wiggin, who fancied himself as an artist, gave the sanctuary his all too undivided attention.

What had been begun by Clayton and Bell he set about completing, and he smothered the walls with insipid paintings in oil and tempera. No doubt it was all done with the best of intentions, in imitation of medieval practice; but it was a grave mistake, which today would be prevented by the diocesan advisory committee. The parish later invited funds for the removal of the vicar's handiwork, but insufficient money was forthcoming. The paintings remain as a curiosity, and doubtless have their champions. The overall effect is not quite as horrific as might be expected, but St George is no longer a Norman church. If anyone needs to be convinced of this, let them go to Elkstone and judge for themselves.

A LOT OF TRAFFIC passes through the village on the B4058 just below the ridge which carries the main road between Gloucester and Bath. Much of the domestic building is of the seventeenth century, clustering prettily near the church of St Martin. The most impressive house is Horsley Court (**118**), approached through dignified gate-posts with balls on top. It has six bays, three either side of a three-storey porch, an oddity, if not unique. Aesthetically this tower-house with its hipped roof is something of an accretion, and does nothing for the façade of the house, but it makes an irresistible picture from the road and is a landmark for the village. In the garden is a seventeenth-century square dovecot.

There are now no traces of the early priory which was established near the present site of the church. The medieval church, too, has largely disappeared with only its Perpendicular tower, robust and with small crocketed pinnacles, remaining. What the visitor now sees is the work of Thomas Rickman, 1838–9, and the masonry, probably of the local Nailsworth stone, is superb. Rickman was a Gothicist who designed with considerable assurance; his most

Hampnett

GLOUCESTERSHIRE
OS 163 101157
1 mile north-west of Northleach

The paintings are based on French Romanesque c. 1150

Horsley

GLOUCESTERSHIRE
OS 162 839980
1½ miles south-west of Nailsworth

Horsley Court

famous building is the New Court of St John's College, Cambridge, and there are over sixty churches, mostly in the Midlands, to his credit. It was he who first classified architectural details in the terms of Early English, Decorated and Perpendicular, a useful shorthand that alone earns him a place in the reference books. His choice of stone is invariably excellent and his buildings are always worth a visit.

Inglesham

WILTSHIRE
OS 163 205984
1 mile south-west of Lechlade

INGLESHAM, though you would scarcely realize it, is on the River Thames, a little over a mile above its last lock. It is no more than a couple of houses, a farm and a church, standing in a grey limestone huddle. The church of St John the Baptist is irresistible. In origin it is 700 years old, and nothing appears to have changed since 1700. That it should be so 'unrestored' is a debt we owe to the Society for the Protection of Ancient Buildings who repaired it in 1888–9 'through the energy and with the help', as the inscription reads, 'of William Morris who loved it'.

So light was the touch of his architect, J. T. Micklethwaite, that you would scarcely sense he had been here; this is the quintessential ancient English parish church – crumbly, uneven floors, medieval wall paintings, oak screens, fragments of glass, a north door with exceptionally long hinges, an Elizabethan pulpit, and high Jacobean box pews with carved friezes. The sculpture of the Virgin and Child, under the hand of God, is pre-Conquest. The bodies are in profile, the heads full face. The child sits on his mother's lap, knees tucked up, a tiny hand tugging at her sleeve, touching in its humanity.

Despite the efforts of liturgical populists, these walls are forever impregnated with the prayers of the faithful when Christendom was one, and the later measured sonority of Cranmer and King James: early church and rural matins for the dwindling few. If ever you wanted to introduce someone to the spirit of the English parish church in its calm, its continuity and simplicity, there could be no better place to begin. Nothing can our peace destroy.

Kelmscott

OXFORDSHIRE
OS 163 250990
3 miles east of Lechlade

MOST VISITORS will come to Kelmscott (pronounced Kems-cot, and sometimes spelt without the final 't') as pilgrims, for William Morris made the manor house his country home from 1871 to 1896. Morris enjoys a special place in the history of English art and aesthetics; he was a major figure in what became the Arts and Crafts movement, and it was he, more than any other, who pioneered an appreciation of the Cotswolds. In 1877, provoked by Sir George Gilbert Scott's plans for the restoration of Tewkesbury Abbey and other over-zealous schemes elsewhere for 'skinning a church alive', he founded the Society for the Protection of Ancient Buildings, with a manifesto which was to rally some of the most influential and eminent people of his time.

The manor house, which is shown by written appointment, is small and unpretentious. It is in the traditional vernacular style, built about 1600 and extended a century later. It is of grey stone surrounded by barns and high trees, some sadly now victims of elm disease, in the flat and still remote upper reaches of the Thames. The house retains much of its charm. It has mullioned windows, some with triangular pediments, gables and ball finials above. The guttering is of wood, and the roof of Cotswold stone slates, expertly graded with the largest at the eaves diminishing in size to the smallest at the ridge. Morris's famous and much quoted phrase with regard to these roof slates bears repeating: 'it gives me the same sort of pleasure in their orderly beauty as a fish's scales or a bird's feathers.' Exactly.

William Morris and his extraordinarily beautiful wife Jane, subject of some of Rossetti's best portraits and object of more than his passing attentions, furnished the house with simple but solid chairs and tables, tapestries, carpets, wallpapers and murals designed by Morris himself and Ford Madox Brown. The tiles in the grate were executed by William de Morgan from Morris's designs. 'Have nothing in your houses', Morris said in one of his many aphorisms, 'that you do not know to be useful or believe to be beautiful.' The restoration of the house in 1968, necessary no doubt and certainly expensive, has produced an interior devoid of clutter, well ordered but a little lacking in soul.

Nevertheless there is much to enjoy: furniture, textiles, wallpapers, paintings by Rossetti and Burne-Jones, manuscripts and books from the Kelmscott Press which Morris himself founded, and which in eight years produced more than fifty books requiring over 600 separate designs for initials, title pages, borders and other adornments. It is a monument to a prodigious energy and achievement; a life dedicated to the pursuit of craft and beauty.

The village straggles between the manor house and the church nearly half a mile to the north. Even the attractions of Jane Morris could not sufficiently distract Rossetti from his boredom with the village which he described as 'the doziest dump of old grey beehives'. Farmhouses abound and show a variety of date and development from gables to pediment and parapet. Morris is commemorated at the Village Hall. The architect was Ernest Gimson; it was completed in 1934 in the Arts and Crafts tradition. Philip Webb designed the Morris cottages, built at the expense of Morris's wife as another memorial to her husband. On the front is a relief of Morris seated under a tree, carved by George Jack from a sketch by Philip Webb.

Morris is buried with his wife in the south-east corner of the churchyard. The lettering on his tomb, a design by Philip Webb, is fine but badly weathered. The church of St George is small and simple, on a cruciform plan without a tower. A gabled bellcote suffices. For the most part it is a Norman church with Early English transepts, and a clerestory added when the roof was heightened in the fifteenth century. The window at the west end, a design of three grouped foliated lancets, repeated at the south window of the chancel and again in the south transept, dates from the late thirteenth century. The lancets are set within recesses under cinquefoil rere-arches, a great enrichment, and a rarity, although there are more at Bampton. There is some wall painting under trefoiled canopies in the north transept, and some fragments of medieval glass, part of a figure of St George on horseback, in the east window. The benches, plain and simple, were designed by Philip Webb.

Kingham

OXFORDSHIRE
OS 163 258238
5½ miles south-west of Chipping Norton

KINGHAM STILL HAS ITS RAILWAY STATION (and a good-looking stone hotel to go with it) on the Oxford, Worcestershire and Wolverhampton railway (the 'Old, Worse and Worse'), opened in 1853. It was once a junction for the cross-country line between Banbury and Cheltenham. The village, about a mile to the north, is spacious, and much undervalued in its attractions, with wide greens, houses of considerable variety, thatch and slate, and cottages of banded limestone (**121**). The walls here have alternate courses of oolite (the lighter grey) and ironstone (a tawny brown).

Banded limestone cottage, Kingham
Medieval chimney-pot, Kingham

Banding of this kind was either used as an economy to make the more expensive stone (usually the oolite) go further, or simply for decorative effect, and in the villages of north Oxfordshire it became something of a local fashion. Only a few hundred yards further south, surrounded by new 'vernacular' estate houses which are not unharmonious and in design are certainly right in colour for the locality, is another curiosity, a medieval chimney. This rare survivor, looking rather like a pepperpot with its vents under a gabled cap, is set in the roof of the rebuilt Manor Cottages.

At the southern end of the village is the church of St Andrew (**122/3**), for the most part Victorian as a result of the restoration of 1852–3, which also introduced some unusual stone pew-ends and

St Andrew and Kingham

The Rectory, Kingham ▷

backs. The roof, 1774, is perhaps the most satisfying feature, but while the church is modest in its attributes, its Rectory (inevitably the *former* rectory, alas) is one of the finest of its kind in Oxfordshire. It is built of ashlar and of excellent proportions, with superb fenestration all in place beneath a hipped roof and prominent bracket cornice, and it has an impressive pedimented doorway approached by a short flight of steps. The interior, if only it could be seen, no doubt does this façade justice in every possible way. This house is superb.

Langford

OXFORDSHIRE
OS 163 249025
4 miles north-east of Lechlade

LANGFORD IS IN THE FLAT COUNTRY of streams that feed the upper reaches of the River Thames. It is an attractive, quiet village. A former chapel is now a surgery, and houses, large and small, are clearly tended with pride. The church of St Matthew has some important Saxon remains; the supposition is that the Saxon work here was carried out after the Conquest by craftsmen whose skill and knowledge extended further afield to artistic centres in England and perhaps even mainland Europe. The tower of three stages is Saxon in its entirety although the parapet and corbel table were added *c.*1200. It is large and gaunt, and visually not very appealing.

At the south porch are two Saxon sculptures, one a relief of the

Crucifixion, with the figures of the Virgin and St John in attendance, reset carelessly in the tympanum over the doorway. The two figures have been transposed: the Virgin, invariably at Christ's right hand, appears on the left, and both she and St John look outwards not inwards; even worse, Christ's arms incline downwards with hands reversed. It is most disconcerting, something like seeing a transparency from the wrong side, and these panels should surely be reset. On the east wall of the porch is Christ Triumphant with arms outstretched, the Langford rood, dated *c*.1000. The representation is life-size and austere. Christ is robed in a tunic with straight sides but sadly the figure is headless. Not much modelling survives, but it is an impressive piece and the horizontal arms with hanging sleeves are most effective. On the south wall of the tower is another relief of two figures also in tunics, with arms upstretched supporting what was once a sundial.

The church was enlarged *c*.1200 when aisles were added, and the nave arcade with its tall round pillars and carved stiff-leaf capitals is of some beauty. About 100 years later the chancel was rebuilt with the same window arrangements, the unusual concave lozenges above paired lancets, that appear at Wyck Rissington. This church has certainly spread its wings. The central tower, however, is so obstructive that the chancel is apparently seldom used, for the high altar is scarcely visible (and the choir stalls never) from most parts of the nave. There is now, rightly, a nave altar to the west of the tower.

Lechlade

GLOUCESTERSHIRE
OS 163 215995
8 miles south-west of Burford

THE TALL SPIRE of St Lawrence beckons across flat lands from Kelmscott and invites the southern exploration of the Cotswolds. The little town stands at the crossing of the Oxford to Cirencester road with the route from Swindon to Stroud and the north, and at the meetings of the Rivers Leach, Coln, and Cole with the Thames at its highest navigable point. Lechlade is a popular marina. The church is almost entirely Perpendicular, with a good tower and spire; it is one of the great Cotswold 'wool' churches, and although many of its features were submerged in the restoration of 1882 by F. S. Waller, and the stained glass is terrible, it presents a light, spacious interior with soaring piers. The ashlar from Taynton is its chief asset. The chancel roof was pleasantly repainted by Patrick Phillips in 1938. The churchyard was celebrated by Percy Bysshe Shelley in his summer-evening stanzas of 1815. 'Here could I hope that death did hide from human sight sweet secrets.'

Lechlade has attractive streets, but sited at the crossing of two busy roads it is far too full of traffic, long vehicles turning and twisting. The town urgently deserves a bypass. The best of the architecture is in Burford Street with Ryton House outstanding. It is built of coursed rubblestone, but has freestone quoins and stands on an ashlar plinth. Further down Burford Street is a convent, formerly Lechlade Manor, set in parkland and seen at a distance from the Faringdon road. It is the work of J. L. Pearson, 1872–3, in his Jacobean mode. St John's Street, Wharfe Lane and High Street are all worth a perambulation.

The gazebo is a speciality of Lechlade, and nearly every self-respecting garden seems to aspire to one of some sort or another. Church House, close by the churchyard, has a particularly impressive example, glimpsed over the wall with difficulty by standing on a tomb-chest, or with a jump. It is built of brick but dressed in stone, and has a Venetian window and a pediment over the entrance. In the market place is the inn, attractive in chequer-patterned brick with stone porch and dressings and the wide glazing bars that indicate an early eighteenth-century date. The old vicarage is close by, much clad in creeper. It was built by Richard Pace who was born in the village and lies buried in the churchyard.

St John's Bridge, half a mile away on the eastern approaches, was recorded as a bridge across the Thames early in the fourteenth century. Two hundred years later Leland noted it as having three arches but it was altered twice in the nineteenth century to accommodate increasing traffic. The parapet and piers of the rebuilding of the 1830s survive. The arch accommodating the lock stream has been thoughtlessly patched in a shiny blue-grey brick. Halfpenny Bridge, built in the eighteenth century with a semi-circular stone arch, provides the crossing from the south, and to the south-west is another bridge, over the Thames and Severn Canal where it makes its junction with both the River Coln and the Thames. A round house, presumably for the maintenance man, and cottage are nearby. They make an enjoyable group, well worth the walk along the river-bank.

Little Washbourne

GLOUCESTERSHIRE
OS 150 989334
5½ miles north-west of Winchcombe

THE HAMLET APPEARS as not much more than a public house on the main A438 road to Tewkesbury, and the traveller, and indeed anybody living in the vicinity, could well be unaware of the existence of St Mary, a chapel of ease.* It is small and secret. It lies 200 yards to the north of the road, yet utterly remote, hidden in an orchard with no graves in the churchyard. It has a nave, a lower chancel, stone roofs and a bellcote in white roughcast. The structure is largely Norman, but nearly everything else, and especially the woodwork, is Georgian, and has remained untouched by later ages. The pulpit, reading-desk and box pews are all in silvery-brown oak. The walls are rendered. The pews are anything but comfortable, and the only lighting is from candles. Who would wish otherwise?

Malmesbury

WILTSHIRE
OS 173 933873
12 miles south-west of Cirencester

WHERE THEN, from the southern approaches, do the Cotswolds begin? Brunel's Great Western and the M4 help set the limits, but not entirely satisfactorily; somewhere, almost imperceptibly, just south of Malmesbury, hedgerows give place to rubblestone walls. At Malmesbury we have surely arrived. The town could equally

* A redundant church. The key is available locally.

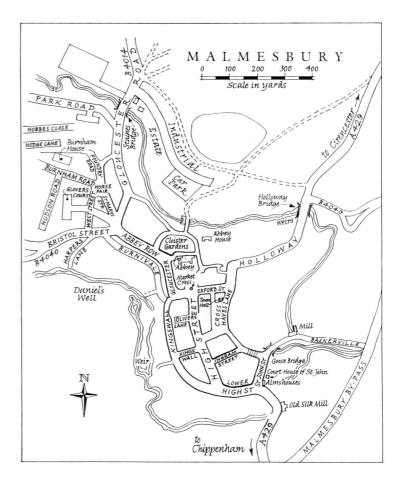

serve as the climax or departure point of any Cotswold journey; to the east lies the Oxford clay and the basin of the upper Thames, to the south the Wessex chalk, full of sheep, to the north and west the promise of oolitic limestone and the Cotswolds in all their beauty.

'The toune of Malmesbyri', wrote Leland in 1542, 'stondith on the very toppe of a greate slaty rok, and ys wonderfully defended by nature'; and its hilltop site, surrounded on almost all sides by the waters of the River Avon and its tributary the Inglebourne, which are crossed by no fewer than five bridges, is one of its great attractions. The Saxons used this natural stronghold to build a castle, beneath whose walls a Celtic monk, Maidulph, set up a religious community. The town lays claim to being the oldest borough in England, from the granting of its first charter by King Alfred in 880.

Its prize possession is the surviving fragment of the former magnificent Benedictine abbey church, the nave of which was saved at the Dissolution by a wealthy clothier, William Stumpe. He bought the abbey from the Crown, demolished most of what remained, and built himself a substantial house with gables and projecting wings, Abbey House, on the foundations of the abbey reredorter overlooking the river. The nave of the abbey, in which he reputedly set up his looms, he gave to the town as its parish church.

The church is built of slightly dour, non-reflecting grey limestone, which nevertheless shows pleasant light buff yellows as well. It was completed about 1181, with later additions at the east and a spire for the central tower; a large, square Perpendicular west tower followed in the late fourteenth century. The crossing tower fell, according to Leland, about 1530, and from the Dissolution all the building east of the crossing was left to decay. This must have been a huge church, bigger and bolder than many cathedrals. The immense arch which still stands dramatically in a garden to the east gives an exciting idea of the scale on which this abbey church was originally built. The Norman west front, which despite all the evidence to the contrary looks as if it were built to sustain twin towers, is richly carved. There is interlaced blank arcading round much of the wall below the aisle and south transept windows. The Decorated additions of the building's second phase are also fine, especially the bold flying buttresses with pinnacles, in the French style, and the lierne vault inside with its large gilded bosses.

The striking feature of the interior is the height, accentuated no doubt because only six of the nine wide and lofty bays survive. The Norman piers are huge but short in comparison with the upper reaches of the triforium and clerestory. The triforium on the south side is interrupted by an odd little fifteenth-century 'watching chamber' which looks more like a hansom cab than anything remotely ecclesiastical. Over the main arches, which mostly have billet ornament, are masks of grotesque animals, lively and effective; at least one is feline in appearance, and others at the ends of the hood-moulds are more horse-like.

The huge Perpendicular west window is a great asset, for the clear glass provides an admirable source of light, and is in marked contrast to the windows of grim, light-defying Victorian glass to the south. In the north-east corner lies the tomb of Alfred's grandson, King Athelstan, whose name lives on in the town in cottage, café, garage and bingo hall. New chairs were dedicated in 1988. They are no doubt more comfortable than those they replaced, and in any event are more welcome than 'town' pews, but their modernity does not suit the church. The wall at the east end of the nave, hiding the ruin beyond, is blank and cries out for ornament. It is a pity that some effective mural, sculpture or tapestry, as a point of artistic focus, has yet to be found.

The south porch is Malmesbury's glory, and one of the most important sculptural ensembles in England (**128**). It is, like the nave, French in feeling, and comparisons with Moissac, Souillac, Autun and Aulnay immediately spring to mind. At the entrance a plain outer arch protects an inner one of no fewer than eight orders. Five are alive with trails and ingenious geometrical devices; three

South Door, Malmesbury Abbey

contain pictorial sculpture not easy to read, set within medallions. From the inner arch emerges the story of the Creation; in the middle we have Noah, Abraham, Moses and David; at the outer arch, scenes from the life of Christ. The carving was cleaned and beautifully restored by the Department of the Environment under the direction of John Ashurst in 1977. The limestone, then almost black, particularly on the outer arch, was so much weathered that even the gentlest jet of water would have been too fierce for such fragile carving. A most delicate abrasive had to be devised, and every tiny detail that had become detached was put back in place on a filler of lime putty and lime-dust. The care was meticulous, the effect astonishing.

The sculpture on the side walls inside the porch is very striking (**129**). It represents six seated Apostles with an angel, horizontal in flight, above. The relief, four inches at a guess, is bold; every pose is different and some of the gestures are extremely mannered. Above the inner door is a tympanum, a Christ in Glory, reminiscent of Autun, set within a vesica. Christ has a small head and long body, and is supported by two elongated floating angels. Around the tympanum and down the uprights are bands of foliage. In a room above are kept four volumes of an illustrated bible dating from 1407.

The churchyard is entered by the Tolsey, the place for the collection of tolls as at Burford and elsewhere. The spire of St Paul's, soaring to the south-west, is all that remains of the original parish church of the town, and provides the abbey with a belfry.

South porch sculptures,
Malmesbury Abbey

Among the graves is commemorated Hannah Twynoy, who died
after being mauled by an escaped tiger from a travelling circus.
From some high point, if the great medieval chronicler William of
Malmesbury is to be believed, Brother Elmer, a monk of the
eleventh century, after fixing himself a pair of wings, essayed a first
attempt at man-powered flight; he flew for more than a furlong
before he flopped. One would like to think that the low-flying jets
on exercise roar past in symbolic salute to an early pioneer.

Further along Abbey Row and beyond in Horsefair, in a house
in its south-east corner now long since demolished, the philo-
sopher Thomas Hobbes was born in 1588. Higgledy-piggledy
houses with stone roofs cling to the hillside, views over the river
convey a feeling of space and a breath of fresh air. This is a good
place to live.

At the centre of the town is the octagonal Market Cross, built
about 1500, superior artistically to Salisbury or Chichester, and
one of the best in England. It has a lierne vault, and at the apex
some attractive sculptures with a delicate Crucifixion on the west
face. It has withstood many a brush with excessively 'long vehicles'
negotiating its vulnerable site. Tower House, at the junction of
Oxford Street with Cross Hayes, closes the view to the east. This
was another of William Stumpe's houses, medieval in origin, with a
hall under a hammerbeam roof where he is said to have entertained
Henry VIII. It is now a private garage. The tower was added by a
star-gazing enthusiast, Dr Player, in the nineteenth century.

St John's Almshouses,
Malmesbury

High Street winds its way down from the Cross to the river. At the bottom are the gabled almshouses, founded in 1694, but incorporating somewhat incongruously a late Norman arch from the former Hospital of St John, whose order was suppressed in 1540. The burgesses bought and adapted the buildings, and established the old Courthouse behind. It has a simple and atmospheric interior, the meeting-place of the old Corporation who claim direct descent from men to whom Athelstan, in a pre-Conquest feudal fling, gave common land in return for help in battle against the Danes. It survives, even in these days of sex equality, as a men-only affair.

By the river is a large former silk mill, the best secular building in the town, four storeys high, with eight bays in each of its L-shaped wings. It stands sentinel in a group with the bridge, making a splendid southern entrance to the town. In April and May daffodils give way to lilac, willow and poplar fringe the meadows, and the limestone glows, reflected in the Avon. Nothing could be more inviting, with the promise of the abbey, focus and *raison d'être* of the town, presiding on the hill above.

Meysey Hampton

GLOUCESTERSHIRE
OS 163 117001
2½ miles west of Fairford

MEYSEY HAMPTON lies just a mile from the Wiltshire border; it is meticulously kept and tidy, with a variety of cottages, houses and stone walls of different shapes and sizes; it has also a manor, a narrow Georgian building of some distinction, overlooking the green. The church of St Mary, consecrated in 1269, cruciform in plan with a central tower, has two great surprises.

James Brooks' restoration of 1872–4 was punitive, but on the south side of the chancel there is a gorgeous Decorated display: a large tomb recess, triple sedilia and piscina, all with richly crocketed canopies. For a parish church in a small village it is something of quite extraordinary magnificence. Equally unexpected, but in a somewhat unsophisticated and flamboyant vein, is the monument in the south transept to James Vaulx, doctor of medicine, who died in 1626. The effigies are life-size, half-length, in painted stone. The

Monument, St Mary,
Meysey Hampton

doctor is depicted with his two wives – the deceased somewhat romanticized, and the living rather less so, plump of face and lank of hair. He holds his head in his hand and looks more than a trifle bewildered.

Mickleton
GLOUCESTERSHIRE
OS 151 163435
3 miles north of Chipping Campden

MICKLETON, a straggling village too much cheek-by-jowl with a through road, is worth a stop on the corner near the church if only for Medford House, built *c.*1694, in the reign of William III. In a village that admits of brick and looks to the Vale of Evesham, this lovely house is faced with a golden ashlar. 'The pediment of the porch and the florid urn above the rounded arch are its concession to seventeenth-century classicism . . .' wrote H. J. Massingham,* 'the mullions and transoms of the windows and the general treatment of the symmetrical front are Cotswold.' The gables have given way to a hipped roof with dormers, yet the house is not square; it is a fascinating example of a slow shift of style and taste, 'the text-book example', as David Verey wrote in his Shell Guide, 'of the transition from Tudor to Queen Anne'.

Alec Clifton-Taylor also admired this house and illustrated it in his indispensable *Pattern of English Building.*† His keen eye alighted on two features: the use of stone, and the pitch of the roof

Medford House, Mickleton

at the eaves. The ashlar of the Cotswold limestone is generally small in size, with the possible exception of Guiting. Except in monumental buildings, excessively large stones, as Pugin observed, destroy proportion; and around Gothic windows in grand churches and cathedrals, smaller stones certainly look much better.

* *Cotswold Country*, Batsford, 1937.
† Revised J. Simmons, Faber, 1987.

Small stones, however, require a lot of mortar which can detract from the quintessential dignity of ashlar. At Medford House, the happy medium is admirably on show: small stones laid with stunning precision in absolutely level courses for the house; larger, less carefully jointed stones for the garden wall adjacent.

A slight change of pitch in the roof is noticeable towards the base. The fall becomes gentler, and the stone slates – even allowing for the usual grading, diminishing progressively from the eaves towards the ridge – become wider. This was achieved by attaching to the rafters, near the lower ends, additional lengths of wood set at a shallower pitch and known as sprocket-pieces. The effect was practical as well as aesthetic. It provides a slight check on the flow of rain water just where it might splash over the gutter. It adds, moreover, a touch of distinction to the formality of the building.

The church of St Lawrence is Norman in origin, with a fourteenth-century tower and a broach spire at the west end. It was restored in 1868; two monuments by Edward Woodward and one by Henry Scheemakers, both of the early eighteenth century, are the only items of note. In the village, which has timber-frame and thatch as well as some very commonplace modern development, is a memorial fountain by William Burges, one of the more flamboyant but enjoyable of Victorian architects. His work, even in miniature, is always worth looking at.

Minchinhampton

GLOUCESTERSHIRE
OS 162 873008
2 miles north-east of Nailsworth

MINCHINHAMPTON, once a prosperous wool town high on the ridge above the River Frome, survives almost unspoiled. It is entirely of the local grey stone, with pretty grouping in every direction. Four straight streets intersect at the Market House, built in 1698 and restored in 1944. It stands on stone columns, with a sprocketed stone roof, and provides a focus in the middle of the town. There are good houses to see in every street: a Post Office from the reign of Queen Anne, and buildings of all sorts and sizes; gables, parapets, finials, vases, ashlar, rubblestone, castellated Gothick, keystones and hood-moulds, even stucco – a whole range of variety and architectural detail (**134**).

To the south the street descends steeply into countryside. On the southern slope known as the Vineyards is Lammas House, built about 1790, with hanging gardens. There are other houses along the terraces, two by Peter Falconer (of a distinguished and well-respected modern practice of Cotswold architects), who built St Francis with its restored gazebo and ice-house for himself. Further to the south-east is Gatcombe Park, built for the Sheppard family of clothiers about 1770, but sold when their fortunes declined to the eminent economist David Ricardo, MP. Ricardo employed Basevi, c.1820, to work for him and the house has not been altered again since then.

The valley below is worth visiting; by the edge of a lake, made by damming the stream as early as 1806, stands Longford's Mill –

Minchinhampton

built, as so much else in these parts, for the making of flannel and
worsteds. Doubtless the working environment was grim and the
hours long, hard and depressingly dull, but these buildings do not
scar the landscape in the way that many later factories were to do.
To the north-west of Minchinhampton large tracts of common
land are safely in the ownership of the National Trust. It is an area
of nearly 600 acres, riddled with round and long barrows, Iron
Age hill-forts and defensive works. 'You must be so good to
tell me', wrote Horace Walpole, 'if there is anything in my way
worth stopping to see – I mean literally to see: for I do not love
guessing whether a bump in the ground is Danish, British or
Saxon . . .' There are dozens of bumps, some historic no doubt,
others the workings of wildlife, and the golf club has also left its
mark.

The parish church of the Holy Trinity is to the north of the
Market Hall and approached by a trim, well-planted churchyard
with some fine tomb-chests and gravestones. There is not one
jarring note. The stone for the church is a buff grey. The central
tower is fourteenth-century; in 1563 it was reduced in height,
truncating its effect, but given a stone coronet which is both pretty
and original. Much of the church is Victorian, resulting from a
restoration of 1842 with alterations twenty years later by William
Burges. The east window, richly conceived with double tracery,
is Burges at his best.

There are two brasses of cadavers in shrouds, and two early
fourteenth-century effigies in tomb recesses. The arms on the

shield suggest the de la Meres, Peter and Matilda, who were probably the donors of the church's most noble feature, the south transept. The buttresses on this exterior, close together and separated by slender Decorated two-light windows, well seen on the way in, have already whetted the appetite. They support the vault, which is really only a pitched roof of stone slates visible from underneath, but crossed in scissor fashion by transverse arches which look like timber but are most unexpectedly made of stone. The *clou*, however, is the glorious south window, a large wheel-like rose full of ogee tracery.

Minster Lovell
OXFORDSHIRE
OS 164 323115
2½ miles west of Witney

MINSTER LOVELL is on the north bank of the River Windrush and reached by a bridge which in origin must be over 500 years old. Here is peace within only a quarter of a mile of the roar of traffic on the A40. Those sent to conferences at the centre recently and successfully converted from the old mill down by the stream must scarcely believe their luck. The village has some thatch and timber-frame. At the Swan Inn, where the roof is on a steep pitch clad in Stonesfield stone slates, the infill between the exposed timbers is roughcast – not in itself attractive, but its texture contrasts well with the rubblestone masonry of the rest of the house. A brook flows by the side of the one straight street down into the Windrush below; the houses are set back and are reached by flat stone-slab foot-bridges.

At the top of the village's gentle rise to the east, cars have to be abandoned for the last few hundred yards' walk to the church and Hall. The more adventurous can find a footpath by the river all the way from the bridge. The church and ruins of the Hall, now tidy and spruce and in the care of English Heritage, stand above the green pastures and water-meadows of the Windrush, surrounded by cow-parsley and grazing cattle. The house, one of the grandest in Oxfordshire, was built by the Lovell family, lords of the manor, *c.*1431–42. They were associates of Richard III, and after his defeat in 1485 their lands were forfeit.* The house continued to be inhabited for another three centuries but then fell into disuse and became farm buildings until its restoration in the 1930s.

The ruins (**137**), in their setting amongst trees and mown grass, are somewhat confused, but with the helpful English Heritage guide in hand the visitor can reconstruct the organization of this large house. To the north is a circular dovecot, and the manor farm which incorporates features of the thirteenth and fifteenth centuries. At the farm and in the garden of the Hall is a medieval cobbled way. The cobbles were gathered, presumably, from the bed of the Windrush, and although not laid, or perhaps relaid, with the

* Anthony Turner has reminded me of the old rhyme:
  The Cat, the Rat and Lovell the Dog,
  Rule(d) all England under the Hog.
  See also Shakespeare's *Richard III*, Act III, Scene 4 – D.M.

greatest artistic skill, they show virtually no sign of wear. They are set in a criss-cross pattern separated by strips of limestone.

The name 'Minster', from the Latin word *monasterium*, derives from the church of St Kenelm which was served by a small priory. It was probably a Norman building in origin, but was rebuilt by William, Lord Lovell, about the time of the house. The church is cruciform with a somewhat squat Perpendicular tower placed at the centre. Inside, the west wall of the tower is supported on two huge piers linked to the nave by narrow arches. The carvings on the pillars include a bishop, a lady (perhaps a Lovell), a crowned head, and another, perhaps the master mason. These piers in effect act as flying buttresses and (an unusual feature) make it possible to see both chancel and transepts simultaneously from the nave.

In the south transept is an alabaster tomb, perhaps William Lovell himself, with heraldic shields recently repainted and jewel-bright. The nave and chancel are almost equal in length. The windows have fragments of old stained glass dating from the second half of the fifteenth century, and almost all the original seating in the nave survives. This is a church with atmosphere and, despite its fairly drastic restoration by J. L. Pearson in the 1870s, it retains much of its medieval feeling. Church and ruined Hall side by side in the tranquil water-meadows: this is the Cotswolds at their most romantic.

Miserden
GLOUCESTERSHIRE
OS 163 935089
6 miles north-east of Stroud

MISARDEN PARK (the spelling is correct), an enormous gabled Elizabethan house much enlarged by Edwin Lutyens in 1920–21, is sited just above the village and enjoys magnificent views over the 'Golden Valley' of the tree-hidden River Frome to the south. The gardens, regularly open to the public, are on a grand scale. Lutyens created a loggia overhung with wistaria, and special features are the extensive yew hedges and the carefully detailed grass steps on a lawn to the south. In the woodland to the north-east are the remains of a motte and bailey, built by the Musard family (an old French nickname meaning 'dreamer'). They gave their name to the locality probably shortly after the Conquest.

The church of St Andrew, well cared for and approached through an arch of yew, was Saxon in origin, but what remained of earlier restorations was swept away in 1866 by the heavy hand of the amateur architect, the Revd W. H. Lowder, who was also rash enough to tamper with the church at Ozleworth. The monuments of the seventeenth century, south of the chancel, are the things to see. A goat eats a cabbage on a fine effigy of William Kingston by Samuel Baldwin of Stroud, but it is hard to admire paint on Cotswold stone. Nor is it easy to sympathize with Derbyshire alabaster, however accomplished the craftsmanship (particularly of the clothes), on the recumbent effigy of Sir William Sandys and his wife Margaret Culpeper, who lived in the Park. The kneeling Partridges in the sanctuary, Anthony and Alice, are also by Baldwin.

Many of the village cottages were designed by Sidney Barnes *c*.1920. They are now highly desirable semis which in texture and neighbourliness suit the locality well, even if they do look a trifle garden-suburb. The Camp is a small settlement of houses and barns to the west. Hazle House is set on top of a hill, striking and unusual, with a central porch and the skyline of its front patrolled by huge lions and eagles. On a by-road branching to the north-west is Whiteway, a colony founded in 1898 by Neville Shaw, disciple of Tolstoy. The inhabitants built their own houses, shared out the land and lived a life of friendly co-operation and self-support, untrammelled, as they hoped, by the intrusions of government. It was a laudably idealistic venture, very much home-grown, high-thinking and plain-living, with assiduous study of the master's novels no doubt thrown in. For most mortals that requires a life of some leisure. Today, the colony has the sad air of a shanty town.

Naunton

GLOUCESTERSHIRE
OS 163 113233
7 miles south-west of
Stow-on-the-Wold

THE VILLAGE straggles along the narrow winding valley of the River Windrush for about a mile just north of the A436 Stow to Cheltenham main road, and only hears but does not suffer the heavy traffic. A number of the houses are modern, including some built by the local authority, and recent buildings, infill and restoration, have, broadly speaking, been sympathetic to the environment. Stone predominates and Guiting is only about two miles away. Naunton was formerly one of those quarries (Eyford and Slaughter close by were others) on a seam west-south-west of Stow that produced stone roofing-slates almost identical in character with the celebrated examples from Stonesfield in Oxfordshire.

These slates occur only in a thin seam, varying from about thirty inches to six feet, and were mined from a depth of about sixty to seventy feet. Of these Gloucestershire mines Naunton was the largest; in its heyday the pits are said to have produced about 30,000 slates a week, and at the turn of the century one pit alone employed 100 men. Demand for Cotswold slates is still buoyant, but production too costly and uneconomic, and re-use is often made of slates stripped from buildings in course of demolition. Where stone-slated buildings have been outside planning controls, the situation has sometimes been ruthlessly and greedily exploited; local authorities should be more vigilant and list and protect these rural roofscapes.

The approach to the village is best from the west. The road descends steeply to the river and then sharply up the other side. In the hollow on the left, easy to miss behind the yews and beech, is the church of St Andrew. It is mostly sixteenth-century, but extensively restored and altered by Waller and Son in 1899. The stone is ashlar. The church has a well-proportioned west tower, simple, but with corner pinnacles and gargoyles. There is no stained glass except for some narrow Victorian borders, and the large yews in the churchyard are framed picturesquely in the east window. The walls inside are heavily ribbon-pointed. There is a Saxon cross set in the north wall of the nave but it is the Perpendicular stone pulpit which is the church's chief treasure. It dates from *c.*1400 and is one of the best in the county, richly carved with tracery, panels, canopies and pinnacled buttresses. The base is modern.

The houses round the church and bridge make a pleasant group, and from the terrace behind the Baptist chapel there is a view across the valley of the Windrush below. In a meadow is a four-gabled dovecot with a central topknot, built about 1600 and restored in 1949. The birds fly in and out through little windows in the gables, but the setting, alas, is seriously marred by scruffy agricultural buildings nearby.

North Cerney
GLOUCESTERSHIRE
OS 163 018078
4½ miles north of Cirencester

THE VILLAGE IS ON THE RIVER CHURN, just about as far to the north of Cirencester as South Cerney is to the south. It is bisected by the river and the main road; the village is to the east and the church, with some nice houses for neighbours, is to the west. The church of All Saints is exquisitely sited, high in its churchyard against a backdrop of trees. A medieval cross with a Victorian topknot stands outside the south transept.

The church was originally Norman, but much rebuilt in the late fifteenth century after a fire which gutted the tower and nave. The masonry is patchy: a fair amount of rubble, old roughcast and lime-plaster. The lower part of the tower is Norman, as is the south door with its diapered tympanum and four curious little heads on the lintel. The church is not small, but the rebuilding of the tower only aspired to the saddleback. There are some impressive gargoyles (notably a muzzled bear) over the north and south doors, and some incised drawings, a large leopard on the south-west buttress of the tower and a manticore (half-man, half-lion) on the south wall of the south transept. These graffiti, which David Verey* suggests are post-Reformation and thereby all the more curious, may have been copied from a bestiary, one of which describes the manticore as having 'the head of a grey-eyed man with three rows of teeth, the body of a lion, and the tail of a scorpion'.

On the jamb of the tower doorway is a mass clock or scratch dial, usually suggestive of a date before the Conquest, and therefore likely to have come from an earlier building. Within, the tie-beam roof is supported on the north side of the nave by three superb corbels: bold portrait heads of Henry VI, with a crown, and of a cassocked cleric, perhaps William Whitchurch, rector at the time of the rebuilding. A third is almost certainly Edward Stafford, duke of Buckingham and lord of the manor. The east window of the south transept has fifteenth-century stained glass, some of it a delectable

* *Gloucestershire: The Cotswolds*, second edition, Penguin Books, 1979.

[139]

blue; the emblem of the house of York, a flaming sun, dates it before Bosworth Field.

The furnishings make a formidable collection. First there is an ancient French processional cross of *c*.1320 in silvered and gilded copper. Next a lectern in the form of a brass eagle, dating from 1480, and the pulpit, one of the best in the county, cut from a single block of stone in the form of a wineglass, something of a Cotswolds speciality. Three small wooden statues of great delicacy on the reredos of the Lady Chapel are also of this date. The Virgin is French, and the bishops Urban and Martin are from South Germany. The gallery, reached by an outside staircase, was built in 1754.

Little wonder that such a treasure-house attracted the eye of F. C. Eden, a sensitive exponent of the Arts and Crafts, and the munificence of his friend, William Ivesome Croome, which made so much of the modern restoration and innovation possible. The rood loft, screen to the Lady Chapel, and reredos are all by Eden (*c*.1924–5) in a greyish oak, and he also designed windows in the south transept, sacristy and gallery, and a vestment. There is much else of minor interest: eighteenth-century communion rails of Norway oak, candlesticks of bronze and sedilia of oak, and funerary lights by Dykes-Bower who also designed the decoration of the organ case.

The best houses are nearly all close by. Old Church House dates from the rebuilding of the church; it stands to the south, above the churchyard, and with the former Rectory makes an attractive group. The Old Rectory was built by John Coxe, the rector, in 1694, with a bow in the Gothick taste added *c*.1828, and a west wing, again the creation of F. C. Eden, extended just before the First World War. Eden also provided the round lodge for Cerney House, a substantial Georgian reworking of an earlier house gutted by fire, which stands surrounded by trees to the west. North Cerney was clearly Eden's earthly paradise.

Northleach
GLOUCESTERSHIRE
OS 163 113146
10 miles north-east of Cirencester

THE TOWN, now bypassed, stands just to the east of the former crossing of the busy Oxford to Cheltenham trunk road and the Fosse Way. At that junction is the old prison (more recently the police station), which now houses an agricultural museum; only the front survives. It was built by the son of a wealthy clothier, Sir George Onesiphorus Paul. As High Sheriff of the county he was appalled at the overcrowded and insanitary conditions in which prisoners were held. He shared the views of John Howard, his opposite number in Bedfordshire, and demanded bread, water, air, washing facilities and an infirmary as the minimum for a humane and reasonable prison routine. 'Imprisonment', he wrote, 'should be a state of continual occupation and complete seclusion, the one to create the habit of industry, the other to force reflection on the mind.'

St Peter and St Paul,
Northleach

Sir George's designer was William Blackburn, reputedly the only architect to win the confidence of John Howard, and the plans combined all the current reformist ideas on the need for segregation, solitary confinement (seen then as corrective rather than retributive), and useful labour. The building dates from 1789, and around that time Blackburn was responsible for no fewer than fifteen important similar establishments, including those at Bristol, Gloucester, Oxford, Lewes, Ipswich, Dorchester, Liverpool and Limerick. Sir George's building, plain and purposeful, justifiably inspires a moment's reflection on early reformist thinking, and indeed on the philosophy of punishment.

Northleach does not have outstanding architecture, although as an ensemble it is always attractive. Its medieval prosperity, however, provided its great glory, the Perpendicular parish church of St Peter and St Paul, which with Chipping Campden and Cirencester is the noblest in the Cotswolds. It is best seen from the south-south-east across the meadows of the Leach, surrounded on its slight eminence by grey stone houses and walls. It makes the other wool churches of the Cotswolds, wrote H. J. Massingham, 'look more like handsome bribes to heaven'.*

The tower is somewhat austere despite its loftiness, for the three upper stages are rather small. The south porch, however, is famous (**141**) and while it is not as sumptuous as Cirencester, the quality of the masonry and detailing is superlative. It has an upper chamber, which might have served a variety of purposes; a safe deposit for books and documents, a treasury, a residence for a verger or sacristan, or a meeting-place. Domestic use is indicated by the chimney-flue hidden in a buttress and surmounted by a pinnacle in the centre of the west wall. The porch is entered through an ogee arch, and to the east and above are niches with images of Our Lady, the Trinity, St John the Baptist and St Thomas of Canterbury. It is a wonder they escaped the desecrations of the iconoclasts. On the walls within are image brackets, one carved with a representation of a cat and a fiddle and three rats. No sign of a cow or moon.

The nave is light and stately, with scalloped octagonal piers in the style of Chipping Campden, which may have been by the same mason, Henrie Winchcombe. His name appears at the base of the south-east column. The stone is partly ashlar, and where it is plaster it is exactly and correctly the stone colour. The large window at the east end of the nave, however, is no asset; it has clear glass, and (a bad Cotswold habit) reveals the west gable of the chancel roof. This roof is painted a pleasant pale blue but the modern liturgical 'improvements' around the nave altar disturb the composition of the east end and are not really worthy of this setting. The large east window, by Christopher Webb, 1963, is weak and not greatly superior to the dreary plain yellow Victorian glass in the nave. The modern seating, designed by Basil Spence and made by Gordon

* *Cotswold Country*, Batsford, 1937.

Russell, has short backs and is not at all comfortable, perhaps to discourage soporifics; visually, rush-seat chairs are infinitely preferable. But in this magnificent church, these are minor quibbles.

There is a pretty stone pulpit dating from the fifteenth century, and an unusual late fourteenth-century font showing demons cast out through baptism to the accompaniment of an angel band. The Perpendicular sedilia are well preserved and the high altar, sympathetically designed with riddel posts by F. E. Howard, once displayed a rich frontal by Comper. There is a remarkable collection of wool merchants' brasses, not all of which are well preserved. John Fortey (died 1459), who rebuilt the nave and added the clerestory, is perhaps the best example, although in a complete state his kinsman Thomas, renovator of churches and roads, who predeceased him by twelve years, would perhaps have been even more impressive.

The churchyard is large, well kept and has a number of exceptionally good Georgian tombs, both chests and gravestones. After striking twelve noon, the chimes of the church clock rend the air with a performance of *Hanover* – a tune ascribed to Dr Croft, 1678–1727, and generally sung to Sir Robert Grant's 'O worship the King, all glorious above', written some 100 years later. Connoisseurs of school assemblies will remember this is an eight-line hymn; the church clock treats us to three verses every three hours – quite a carry-on!

Notgrove
GLOUCESTERSHIRE
OS 163 109199
3 miles west of Bourton-on-the-Water

NOTGROVE is a remote, straggling and sequestered village, with the church at the far end to the south and quite difficult to find. The Manor House, much rebuilt after a fire, retains its Cotswold sympathies. A dovecot and farm buildings, mostly in stone but with some disagreeable roofing materials, group around the church of St Bartholomew. This is a rather amorphous building, with a west tower and a bulging octagonal spire. The east wall is windowless and in a niche there is a small, crude and much worn crucifix of Saxon origin. Cotswold slates only survive on the south side of the roof; to the north they are of concrete, although nearly the right colour.

The church was dramatically restored in 1873 by J. E. K. Cutts. The walls were scraped, leaving the fabric unsightly; the north aisle was rebuilt, as were the south wall of the chancel and the south door. The three-bay Norman arcade between the nave and the north aisle survives with another example of wide scalloped capitals. This is a dark interior. There is no window at either the east or west end; the poor Victorian glass, in what windows there are, conspires to keep light out, and the large and closely surrounding trees only make matters more difficult. In the porch is a medieval stone coffin, and elsewhere five effigies, nothing much to look at, but historically connected with the family of the thrice-celebrated Dick Whittington.

The east end is filled with a colourful tapestry designed by Colin Anderson, elder son of the manor and grandson of Elizabeth Garrett, who founded the hospital for women in London. It was finished in 1954. It covers and depicts the medieval reredos of the church, the remains of which, showing green and red paint, survive hidden behind. Notgrove church is shown in the surrounding landscape, full of flowers, trees and animals. The tapestry, a most attractive and unusual piece, was woven locally by three generations of the Anderson family and by local parishioners.

A Virgin and Child, glass of *c.*1300, is set in the vestry window to the north. It is a beautiful miniature, a mere eleven inches high, but almost without colour, only white, black and a little yellow, badly worn and corroded. The drawing of the Child is touching and delicate, but Mary appears much better from the outside, and the question arises of whether this was intended, and whether the setting may be the wrong way round. Even so, this is a rare opportunity to see a precious fragment close at hand.

Oddington

GLOUCESTERSHIRE
OS 163 235256
3 miles east of Stow-on-the-Wold

ODDINGTON LIES JUST WEST of the Oxford to Worcester railway line. An old map marks a stream by the church 'Odyn', and shows it draining into the River Evenlode half a mile to the west. The original village was abandoned by the eighteenth century and left its church, St Nicholas, solitary on a little hill at the end of a lane which becomes the bridle-path to Bledington. The church is surrounded by trees and has strong emotional appeal.

The south aisle was once the nave, and the ringing chamber to the east, approached through a massive Norman arch, was formerly the chancel. This was the original church, but about 1240, when it was in the hands of the archbishopric of York, the present nave was created to the north by piercing the wall of the original building with an arcade. The tower was added to the west. In the 1860s, when the present village had established itself with a new Victorian church, St Nicholas became derelict until its rescue in 1912 by the rector, whose work was continued after the First World War by the Society for the Protection of Ancient Buildings.

The chief object of pilgrimage is the late fourteenth-century Doom painting which unusually fills the north wall of the nave. More often Dooms appear above the chancel arch. This one was only revealed in 1913 when much of the dust, dirt and whitewash which had covered it for two centuries was carefully removed by Mr E. T. Long. Between 1969 and 1974 further delicate consolidation was undertaken, financed by the Pilgrim Trust. The colours are mostly red and white and red on white, and the scene is familiar. Christ sits in judgement; angels summon the dead with their trumpets; the righteous approach the castellated towers of Paradise, while the reprobate are dragged by demons to an inferno, where a devil fans the flames with bellows. Fire and brimstone are not enough: a cauldron is on the boil, a gibbet does brisk work, and the hangman, a horrible monster, evidently relishes his gruesome task. But perhaps it is only so much medieval comic cuts; one just fellow is given a helping hand by an angel as he clambers up the battlements of Heaven. The heavenly city, surprisingly for lime-stone country, is of brick. The artist maybe was not a local man, or was inspired by a Continental painting; or perhaps he had seen some of the early brickwork of the East Riding of Yorkshire and wanted to give a boost to the new materials, but it seems unlikely.

The Jacobean pulpit, in which during the dereliction a vixen is said to have raised her cubs, is well carved, perky and placed on a pedestal. It comes complete with tester. The altar and communion rails also have attractive woodwork, and in the porch is a stone bench marked by doing service, it is said, as an arrow-sharpener. The porch has a large mass dial.

In the village are some substantial houses, one of brick. The rectors seem to have done themselves particularly well; in recent years the Rectory was an old manor house, small but comfortable, but earlier the incumbent's domain ran to a farmhouse and barns as well. They make a sizeable group, rubblestone for the farmhouse and roughcast for the Old Rectory itself. The church of the Holy Ascension, 1852, is of little account; it is a cause for regret that in the nineteenth century a short walk to the ancient parish church was considered too inconvenient. Now at last, while not in regular use, St Nicholas is open in the summer months, and has the loving care it deserves.

Owlpen

GLOUCESTERSHIRE
OS 162 799984
3½ miles east of Dursley

OWLPEN IS A PARISH of only about fifteen houses; its church, manor house, mill and barn form an outstanding group prettily situated in a deep combe of the River Cam, which gives its name to the Gloucestershire Cambridge to the west. Owlpen Manor is enchanting (**146**). The entrance is on the south, approached by semicircular steps from the road. The stone is grey in colour and the roofs are perfect; they sag here and there, but it all adds to the romantic appeal. The house is best appreciated from the higher ground to the south as, from other angles, huge yews tend to crowd the site. The centre is roughcast, with ashlar at either side. The exact date is obscure, but is probably early Elizabethan – the chimneys are set diagonally to the axis of the roof, a favourite practice of that period. The remodelling of 1720, which included the insertion of sash windows, consorts not too happily for the purists.

To the south-west is a 'yew parlour', a square space surrounded by yews which must be over twenty feet high. They mask a little stone building which serves as a gazebo or garden room, roughcast but with gables and a fine stone roof. The house can occasionally be visited by parties on written appointment. There are some delight-ful furnishings, Tudor, Stuart, Queen Anne and Georgian, and nothing self-consciously 'on show'. This is a 'homely' house, loved and enjoyed by its lucky owners.

The Manor, hard to believe, was abandoned for about seventy years until 1926. Owlpen House, a Victorian Italianate confection, arose to take its place, but it only survived a century and was demolished in 1955. The stables, with a turret, cupola and ponderous archway, are the only evidence left. Time and taste have taken their rightful toll. The church of the Holy Cross is essentially a Gothick reworking of 1828, with coursed hardstone walls. The interior was systematically spoilt in various restorations between

Owlpen Manor, Uley

1875 and 1913, and the tower was rebuilt during this time. The church is therefore not specially attractive, but it is vital to the ensemble.

Ozleworth

GLOUCESTERSHIRE
OS 162 794933
4 miles east of Wotton-under-Edge

OZLEWORTH BOTTOM, and the settlements associated with it along the stream of the Little Avon, are the Cotswolds at their most secret. The valley is best explored on foot, starting two miles or so to the east at Newington Bagpath (815948) on the map). There was once a castle here; only the dry moat remains, and the church, Norman in origin and dedicated to St Bartholomew, is built of tufa. It was altered in the fourteenth century and S. S. Teulon rebuilt the chancel in 1858. It only ever had a few farms and cottages for customers, and is now bolted and boarded up, forlorn yet romantic, surrounded by its graveyard of towering nettle and rampant bramble.

Half a mile to the south is Lasborough, with its manor house and the church of St Mary (1861–2, by Lewis Vulliamy) sharing enchanted isolation on the side of the valley. James Wyatt's toy fort at Lasborough Park (1794), seen on the hill opposite, is rectangular and embattled, with a tower at each corner. Boxwell – scarcely more than farm, large house and church – is a further mile down the valley, approached (if you come by car) by a drive marked 'Private' and surrounded by the box-tree woods which give the hamlet its name. The church of St Mary is thirteenth-century, and is remarkable for its bellcote, large and top-heavy with an octagonal spirelet, and almost identical (though with less detail) to the one at Biddestone in Wiltshire, south of Castle Combe. Boxwell Court, somewhat lumpish and terrestrial behind, refuses to be outdone by Lasborough and has its own toy-fort entrance.

This exploration is best negotiated on foot with a 2½-inch walkers' map, but even motor access to Ozleworth needs attentive navigation. It is a scattered parish of farms and pairs of cottages, and the church of St Nicholas hides at the end of the curving drive that leads past the pillared entrance of Ozleworth Park, a large eighteenth-century house with later additions, set amid acres of mown grass. The church is much in the back pocket of the big house. It is screened by trees and set in a circular churchyard, which may mark a prehistoric site. Even if this is fanciful, the location certainly is loaded with mystery and has an unkempt attraction, rural and remote.

The church is Norman, and its oldest part is a centrally placed but irregularly hexagonal tower, with a longer wall to the east than to the west – most unusual if not unique. Mutter has been made that it may not have been built as a church at all, but rather as a hunting-lodge for the Berkeley lords of the manor. It has acquired a painted cap and weathercock. The roofs have stone slates, but the walls are of rubblestone and have been overpointed, making it all look a little too trim. Inside, through a low, plain and spreading arch to the east of the crossing, is the chancel, extended in the fourteenth century. By contrast, a pointed, highly decorative and skilfully executed thirteenth-century arch opens on to a short nave, which nevertheless acquired an extra twelve feet at the hand of the Revd W. H. Lowder in 1873. There is little to enjoy inside and the medieval effect is diminished by shiny Victorian tiles and indifferent glass. It is now safely with the Redundant Churches Fund.

Newark Park, a mile to the west, was an Elizabethan hunting lodge and is a recent acquisition of the National Trust. It has a magnificent situation with views towards Bath, the Vale of Berkeley, the Severn Bridge and South Wales beyond. The stone reputedly came from Kingswood Abbey after the Dissolution; the house is in the style of Robert Smythson, the renowned Elizabethan mason-architect who worked at Wollaton Hall in Nottinghamshire and Hardwick Hall in Derbyshire. It was modified in the 1790s by James Wyatt who gave the south front its Gothick air and added the large porch and parapet. Its rehabilitation owes much to the inspiration and unflagging effort of the present tenant.

Painswick
GLOUCESTERSHIRE
OS 162 867097
4 miles north-east of Stroud

THE SOARING SPIRE of St Mary (**149**), erected in 1632, twice struck by lightning and twice rebuilt in the two centuries that followed, lures the traveller to Painswick from every direction; up the hill from Stroud, down the hill from Cheltenham. It is best seen from across the valley at Bull's Cross (OS 162 877087) on the road up from Slad, made known to many by Laurie Lee and his *Cider with Rosie*. The view from the balcony of the Squash Club is spectacular. The dramatic, hilly site is one attraction of Painswick; the limestone, quarried on Painswick Hill a mile or so away to the north, is the other. It is an excellent stone, white when first cut but weathering to grey with exposure, and was used extensively at Gloucester Cathedral and in the surrounding villages.

Painswick, for most of its visitors, means the parish churchyard, one of the sights of England. It was planted about 1792, with ninety-nine yews, whose meticulous annual clipping is followed on the third Sunday in September by an ancient folksy ceremony. These yews are a counterpoint to the superb array of tomb-chests, memorials and tombstones (**151**). Four important factors have contributed to the appearance of this fine burial ground. Painswick was prosperous on account of its wool and its quarries (prosperous people made a point of affording suitably dignified memorials), and stone was near at hand. There was also a talented family of masons, the Bryans, active throughout the eighteenth century. John, 1716–87, son of the founding father Joseph, designed and carved the gate-piers at the north-east entrance to the churchyard, and lies described as 'carver' in a pyramidal tomb to the south.

St Mary, Painswick ▷

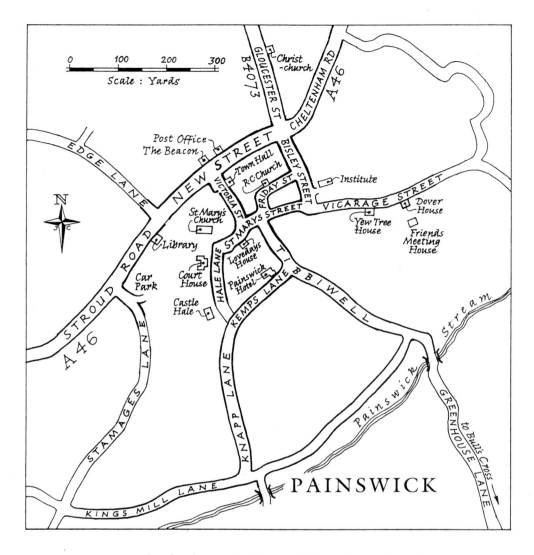

Lastly, almost all of Painswick's tombs are Georgian, the great age – perhaps the only age – of the English churchyard as a work of art.

The church of St Mary is large, and dates mainly from the fifteenth century. It is almost a *Hallenkirche* on the south side, with a wide nave and aisles of equal height. There is not much interest within, and the new porch, added on the south side in 1968 and aslant to the axis of the church, while no doubt useful as a lobby and in reducing draughts, is architecturally something of a disfigurement.

The village, more a little town, has an exceptional range of buildings, and round almost every corner there is something to enjoy. Much of the best is near the church and in the narrow streets to the north and east. New Street unfortunately carries the main Cheltenham–Stroud road, but here The Beacon, Palladian-proud with its parapet, a trifle dowdy but still the grandest house in town, has pride of place. Ashlar in Painswick, as

Tomb-chests and topiary, St Mary, Painswick

elsewhere in the Cotswolds, often masks an earlier timber-framed building, but only the Post Office nearby dares show its inner self, and seems quite a stranger here.

South of the church cluster the larger houses, Court House, Castle Hale, and the Painswick Hotel, approached from Tibbiwell Street. The main interest lies, however, in the more domestic houses, terraces spilling away down the hill, sometimes rubble-stone, sometimes ashlar, hugger-mugger, homely and always appealing, if it weren't for the traffic. Bisley Street, with its early medieval houses, and Vicarage Street are specially attractive.

Two houses, somewhat alike, particularly catch the eye. Loveday's House (**152**), formerly the vicarage, to the east of the church, has all the appearances of a house built, as so many were, from the pattern-books. It is reminiscent of similar houses to be seen, for example, in Stamford, Lincolnshire. It has rusticated quoins, ground-floor windows with Gibbs surrounds, fluted pilasters at the doorway, a Doric frieze and segmental pediment above, and modillion eaves and cornice; it is built in fine ashlar and roofed with stone slates. It is a pity it lacks glazing bars; in such an important position, it should be allowed to look its best. By contrast, Dover House (**153**), down the hill in Vicarage Street, *c*.1720, is all correct, although the effect is best seen with the windows closed. It

Loveday's House, Painswick

Dover House, Painswick ▷

is a beautiful example of early Georgian architecture, with architraves, lugs and keystones at the windows, a pedimented doorway, rusticated quoins, and a cornice similar to Loveday's House.

Painswick has mills in the valley, some fine isolated houses in the surrounding districts, and on all sides views across lush green fields to wooded slopes; a day in Painswick is a day to remember.

Poulton

UNTIL THE END OF THE LAST CENTURY, large quantities of limestone roofing-slate, coarser than the famous Stonesfield from Oxfordshire or Collyweston from Northamptonshire, were available from the Forest Marble, both in the Forest of Wychwood (hence the name) and especially at a number of quarries south of the Burford to Cirencester road. Poulton was one. The village is on the main route from Oxford to Gloucester, and while dog-leg bends at either end slow the traffic, they do not diminish it. The Manor House, an attractive, neat, square, two-storey building of c.1680, suffers particularly from being right on the main road. The village is pleasing and compact, and all in stone.

The church of St Michael, as indeed the school close by, now a private house, is by William Butterfield. The date is 1873, so the discerning visitor must fear the worst, but as it is in stone, not brick, polychrome is not the order of the day. The church is bordered by yews, and has a typical Butterfield belfry with no tower. The interior is spacious and restrained, with a wide nave and an aisle to the north. Six of the windows have rere-arches with pretty cinque-foiled heads, and no jazzy patterns intrude save in the floor tiles of the chancel. The Vicarage, by Ewan Christian, which suits the ensemble well, is five years earlier.

Poulton Manor

Quenington

GLOUCESTERSHIRE
OS 163 148039
2½ miles north of Fairford

THE VILLAGE, whose name means 'the women's tun' (or field), lies on the River Coln. The church of St Swithin is down by the river, in a lovely setting with bridge, rectory and mill. At Quenington Court, close by, a gatehouse well over 600 years old survives. It belonged to the preceptory of Knights Hospitaller which owned this site, and in the garden there is a dovecot, which may be of the same date, complete with its revolving ladder for the keeper to reach the birds. The churchyard is largely devoid of gravestones, but the two late seventeenth-century barrel-topped table tombs still *in situ* are a valuable ornament. The church has a Victorian bellcote which appeared in a restoration of 1882 by F. W. Waller, the Gloucester Cathedral architect. It is octagonal and has a candle-snuffer roof.

There are no aisles, but the church has two amazing Norman doorways. The one to the north is unusually rich. It has three orders with chevrons, round mouldings and limpet-shells. On the capitals each side, amid stars, shells, cable and billet, a Jack-in-the-Green, symbol of fertility, appears with foliage issuing from his mouth. The subject of the tympanum is the Harrowing of Hell. The carving, on a single block of local stone, leaves blank areas to either side but is full of life. Christ pinions the Devil with his cross-staff and rescues souls with an outstretched arm. A face, perhaps representing God, appears in a sun-disk above.

The doorway to the south is at first glance more effective though it has sadly had to be protected by an unsightly glass contraption. On closer inspection, however, the tympanum, the subject of which is the Coronation of the Virgin, seems too crowded and lacks vitality. Nevertheless, on a small, out-of-the-way village church two such doorways are of the greatest interest.

The Rissingtons

GLOUCESTERSHIRE
2 miles east of Bourton-on-the-Water

THESE THREE VILLAGES, Wyck (although the Ordnance Survey has it 'Wick'), Little and Great, lie on a north–south line half-way between the ridge and the course of the River Windrush to the west. The approach is best made from south to north on a walk of about four miles, entirely away from roads.

Great Rissington

OS 163 196172

AT GREAT RISSINGTON a manor, farmhouse, church and rectory are at the south-west corner of the village. It would be a pleasant group, but undistinguished modern buildings intrude, and elsewhere the spread of Marley tiles in the 1960s, before more sensitive stone substitutes became readily available, detracts from the ensemble. This notwithstanding, there are many attractive houses, especially the Manor and Rectory which are approached by an avenue of limes. There are plentiful spacious greens, but the church of St John the Baptist, twelfth-century cruciform in origin, has been much Victorianized. The main feature is the broad central tower, the lower stages of which date from *c*.1200, but with battlements and pinnacles of the fifteenth century.

Little Rissington

OS 163 189199

LITTLE RISSINGTON is a mile and a half to the north. The church, dedicated to St Peter, stands apart from the village, and only the top of a low, small tower at the north-west corner reveals itself on the footpath approach. Remote and tranquil, it is set on a little hill bounded by fields, providing a wide vista. The exterior is uninviting, rubblestone with rock-faced masonry at the west end and south porch. The south door is *c.*1200. The arcade between the nave and the north aisle has two broad, low Norman arches with spreading scallop capitals, but at the chancel the Victorians have destroyed much of what there might have been to see. A low side-window has been explained as enabling the sanctus bell to be rung outside the church before a special turret was provided. Villagers unable to attend church were expected to cross themselves and say a prayer when they heard the bell.

The west window, with a simple design of coloured glass, is dedicated to those who died in the service of the Royal Air Force, which has an airfield on the ridge two miles to the south-east. Part of the churchyard to the east is devoted to their graves. The memorials are in Portland stone, designs with good lettering, reminiscent of some of Lutyens' Commonwealth cemeteries in France. The effect is of military regularity, but the area has dignity and is beautifully cared for. To read the ages of these young men is almost unbearably poignant.

Wyck Rissington

OS 163 193215

WYCK RISSINGTON, one and a half miles further on, is the best village of the three. The cottages overlook a duck-pond, the green is wide, and there is a good-looking conversion of a barn close to the church. St Laurence, a familiar dedication along the Fosse Way, is certainly the most rewarding church. The grey-fawn walls are mottled with lichen, and the roof is on an extremely steep pitch. The tower is ill-proportioned, without ornament, and has a poor parapet, but the east end of the chancel is the really unusual, if not remarkable, feature. The windows with their concave lozenges above paired lancets occur also at Langford in Oxfordshire.

The interior has, like the other Rissingtons, been sadly Victorianized, but the limewashed walls and trussed rafters of the roof look well, and in the lancets in the chancel there are fragments of an early fourteenth-century stained-glass Christ Crucified. The church is all the better for the removal in 1879 of the north and south transepts which were added only fifty years earlier. The reredos is a memorial to a parishioner who won a Victoria Cross in the Great War. Twelve carved limewood plaques, said to be sixteenth-century Flemish, illustrating the mysteries of the Gospels, hang on the walls of the chancel. There was once a maze, representing the pilgrim's life and constructed by Canon Cheales, incumbent 1946–79, in the rectory garden. It was bulldozed out of existence when the house was sold off in 1980. *O tempora, o mores!*

Gustav Holst had his first professional engagement in this church as organist in 1892–3 when he was eighteen, and his Opus 8, unpublished, was a 'Cotswold Symphony' composed in 1900. In 1921 he went on a walking tour of the Cotswolds with Ralph Vaughan Williams who was born in Down Ampney, and whose flowing melody of that name (set to 'Come down, O Love Divine') is one of the most beautiful in the canon. He and Holst both drew great inspiration from this English countryside. There are photographs of them together; sympathetic company in a sympathetic landscape.

Saintbury

GLOUCESTERSHIRE
OS 150 117396
4 miles west of Chipping Campden

A MEDIEVAL CROSS on the Cheltenham road marks the turning; if it is a clear day, Saintbury should on no account be missed. The church of St Nicholas is magnificently sited high above a small collection of houses, and is approached only by a footpath (**161**). From the churchyard there is one of the most exhilarating panoramas in the Cotswolds, stretching beyond Bredon to the Malverns some twenty-five miles away. The church is cruciform, but the tower rises to the south, over the transept. The walls of the church are rubblestone, the tower less coarse, and the broach spire ashlar; the higher, the smoother. A gilded weathercock rules the roost.

Inside, the nave and chancel are rendered and whitewashed, and the transepts scraped of their plaster. In the south transept, the ringing chamber of the tower, is an octagonal dole table, quite a rarity, made of stone and presumably used for the distribution of alms. There is a variety of woodwork: parts of a medieval screen, Laudian altar rails, eighteenth-century pulpit and pews with some Gothick in the panelling. The Campden Guild showed their handicraft here and provided wagon-roofs with gilded bosses to the chancel and north transept. C. R. Ashbee's wrought-iron chandelier is the centrepiece. Step out into the churchyard and admire the view. Saintbury is worth the journey for that alone.

Sapperton

GLOUCESTERSHIRE
OS 163 947035
5 miles west of Cirencester

THE BROAD RIDE of Cirencester Park passes half a mile to the south of Sapperton; only those 5,000 gloriously green acres separate the village from the town. In 1900 Lord Bathurst lent Daneway House, west of the village, to Ernest Gimson and the Barnsley brothers, Ernest and Sidney, for their workshop and showroom. Their impact was considerable; traditional materials fashioned by the skills of traditional craftsmen with all the revivalist zeal of the Arts and Crafts movement. Daneway House is private and can only be glimpsed when the trees are not in leaf, clinging to the side of the hill above the River Frome. The setting is perfect.

Nearly everywhere in the village itself the sensitive skills of Gimson and the Barnsleys are to be seen, both in the cottages on the green and in the larger houses. Upper Dorvel was built by Ernest Barnsley himself, and Beechanger by Sidney. The Leasowes was Gimson's creation, and originally had a roof of thatch. All three men are buried in the churchyard in tombs with engraved brass plates, continuing a series which goes back to 1687.

The church dedicated to St Kenelm, whose shrine was at Winchcombe, has a medieval tower placed just east of the crossing. The church, however, in a fine buff-coloured ashlar, dates largely from the reign of Queen Anne, *c*.1705. Most of the windows are round-headed and some retain greenish glass of the period. There is an abundance of Jacobean woodwork: box pews with unusual Atlas bench-ends, an oak cornice in the nave, and panelling in the south transept and the gallery, all brought here from Sapperton House when it was destroyed by the first Lord Bathurst in 1730. The transepts are choc-a-bloc with memorials. Sir Robert Atkyns, the Gloucestershire historian and antiquarian, who rebuilt the church so sumptuously and who died shortly afterwards in 1711, is commemorated, book in hand, to the south; to the north, Sir Henry Poole, who died in 1616, kneels with his family under a huge canopied tomb in dignified if rather dull Jacobean style. A rector, the Honourable and Reverend Alan Bathurst, has the best, albeit in white marble. He died in 1767 aged 38, and is represented on a scroll blown by the winds. Inspired indeed.

'This interior', wrote H. J. Massingham,* 'is more like the muniment room in a mansion of the most secular of ages than a place of worship . . . the dead are attended with an emblematic court of cherubs, skulls, floral insignia, urns, muses, fates and other damsels with or without robes, carved friezes, inscriptions, coats of arms and iron railings. The squirearchs went to heaven in style.'

Selsley

GLOUCESTERSHIRE
OS 162 829038
2 miles south-west of Stroud

SELSLEY IS FOR PRE-RAPHAELITES. The church of All Saints, sited on a steep hillside and best seen from above, has a long nave and chancel, and at the north-west corner a tall saddleback tower, 107 feet high, unfortunately now roofed with lead, and stained. The patron was Sir Samuel Stephens Marling who is said to have required a church based on one at Marling in the Austrian Tyrol; G. F. Bodley was his architect and gave him more French Gothic than anything else, with the addition of a lich-gate and interior furnishings. Bodley is here at his most self-assured, and he provided William Morris and his school with one of their first chances for stained glass in a church setting. It is this complete set, to the east, south and west, that most visitors come to see.

The colours are moderate, but the series consists mainly of a band of small scenes which do not fill the windows; they seem to lack confidence. The Nativity window in the apse is by Ford Madox Brown; Burne-Jones and Campfield contributed others, Rossetti did the Visitation and Morris himself the Annunciation. The best is the Creation rose-window at the west, designed by Philip Webb, with most of the glass by Morris. Adam leans against a tree with

* *Cotswold Country*, Batsford, 1937.

Eve recumbent in the grass: this is almost semi-abstract form, rich in colour, and the most original item in the collection.

Sevenhampton

GLOUCESTERSHIRE
OS 163 033218
8 miles east of Cheltenham

SEVENHAMPTON DERIVES ITS NAME from a locality of seven wells.* The church of St Andrew is long and low with a modest tower and transepts added about 1500 to a building of 200 years earlier. The stone is of fine quality, a mouse-brown ashlar with plenty of lichen. The tower was inserted by way of internal flying buttresses to the south-west and north-west, an extraordinary and uncommon feature. It also has a lantern, narrow but light, with a delicate tierceron vault high up under the belfry – most unusual in a parish church.

The churchyard is overlooked by the shell of the south wing of the manor house, destroyed by fire. Decaying Georgian tombstones lend an elegiac air. The Vicarage is Victorian in the Tudor-Gothic style, attractive of its kind but with top-heavy bargeboards at the gables. The quiet road from Andoversford to Winchcombe is much to be recommended. In this little-visited part of the Cotswolds, the villages provide unending pleasure in the way they fill and complement the landscape.

Sezincote

GLOUCESTERSHIRE
OS 151 172312
4 miles south-west of
Moreton-in-Marsh

SEZINCOTE, pronounced 'seize-in-coat', is for those who enjoy eccentrics and like a whiff of the Orient. 'A good joke, but a good house too,' wrote D. Talbot Rice. It was designed *c.*1803–5 by Samuel Pepys Cockerell for his brother Sir Charles, who had made a fortune in the East India Company and wanted the life of an English country gentleman, lulled by nostalgia for the mystic East. Hindu motifs decorate the doors; an onion dome (where you might expect a lantern) rises between chimney-stacks capped with Indian frills; *chattris*, umbrella-like minarets, mark the corners of the roof, and the *chujja*, a sort of cornice, projects at the eaves. I once spent a week in Montpezat in southern France in a house designed by a railway official who had retired from service in Indo-China. He built himself a replica of his favourite station complete with platforms, waiting-room and booking-hall. There's no place like a home from home.

The dome and chimneys are of copper. The house is built of a yellow-orange limestone, quarried nearby at Bourton-on-the-Hill, and reputed to have been stained artificially to give it a more realistic Indian hue. A pretty glass orangery curves away behind, and a steeply wooded hill (the *cheine-cote*, hillside of the oaks, from the French *chêne* and the Old English 'cote') provides a scenic backdrop. Within, the house is Greek revival, with all the grand reception rooms on the first floor. The Saloon is more Regency than Georgian, the main bedroom *à la* Soane. A huge four-poster,

* *The Concise Oxford Dictionary of English Place-names*, Eilert Ekwall, fourth edition, OUP, 1960. First published in 1936, this is a mine of information on the derivation of place-names here as elsewhere in this book.

and a convincing *trompe l'œil* by Geoffrey Ghing *c*.1964, match the mood of make-believe.

Humphry Repton landscaped the garden. Pools are an important feature, and a little stream trickles down to the lake. Across this valley Thomas Daniell, the topographical artist of India, whose work is to be seen at the Victoria Museum in Calcutta, designed an exotic bridge in the form of a Hindu temple. For those longing for variety in the Cotswolds, Sezincote is a must. The house much charmed the Prince Regent on a visit in 1807, and is said to have inspired the Brighton Pavilion. English architecture would be far less rich without such levity. (*See also* Lower Swell, p. 178.)

(*See also* Lower Swell, p. 178.)

Sherborne

GLOUCESTERSHIRE
OS 163 169147
4 miles east of Northleach

SHERBORNE, strung out along a valley, takes its name from the brook which rises just north of Northleach. Sherborne Park, just by the church, occupies a large site and virtually divides the village into west and east; at the east end, eleven rows of cottages form a model village, built *c*.1820. One cottage, if you remain patient with a rather bizarre system (who would be a postman?), number 88, has the curious distinction of incorporating part of a Norman church, complete with doorway, tympanum, chevron and zigzag.

Sherborne House is now a school. It was an Elizabethan house, bought by Thomas Dutton in 1551, but the pleasantly informal principal front facing west is the only one preserving any reminiscence of Elizabethan architecture. The stone has yellow patches which suggest that it comes from Guiting. It is possible that Valentine Strong of Taynton worked here on the façades, but most of what can be seen today is by Lewis Wyatt (1777–1853), nephew of the prolific James. He rebuilt the house between 1829 and 1834, keeping the style and some of the masonry, but fell foul of Lord Sherborne who summoned Anthony Salvin to complete the work.

Interest in the church of St Mary Magdalene, a mere appendage of the large house, focuses on the Dutton monuments. The best is to Sir John Dutton, cross-legged and nonchalant of pose, with an elbow resting on an enormous urn. The drapery is admirable. It is by J. M. Rysbrack, signed and dated 1749. The monument by Thomas Burman, signed and dated 1661, to John Dutton, full-length in a shroud with his arm in a sling, and inspired by Nicholas Stone's monument for John Donne in St Paul's (1631), is likewise impressive, and there is a pretty wall tablet to William Napier by John Bacon, signed and dated 1794. James Lenox Dutton is commemorated in the sanctuary in a monument by Richard Westmacott the Elder, dated 1791. An angel holds a medallion of the deceased and his wife, and tramples a gruesome skeleton underfoot. If this figure symbolizes Death, it is horribly life-like.

Lodge Park lies within the parish, across the A40 trunk road, two miles to the south-west. The entrance is grand: two huge piers with banded vermiculation, balls, and distinguished iron gates.

St Nicholas, Saintbury,
Gloucestershire

The twin lodges were added in 1898, suitable in style, but with slate roofs. A short drive, bordered by grass and fruit-trees, leads to the house, which was designed perhaps by John Webb, 1611–72, a pupil of Inigo Jones, and built in grey stone for John Dutton (1598–1657), who was a confidant of Cromwell. It was conceived as two equal spaces with a hall below and room above, the balcony of which would serve as a grandstand for watching deer being coursed by dogs in the park. It was only converted, with much alteration inside and to the rear, into a dwelling-house in 1898. It is an unusual building of some charm. The portico of three bays, the balustrades and the raised-eyebrow pediments, all of which are original to the house, are the special features. The passing visitor will be glad to get a glimpse, if only from the road.

Shipton Oliffe

GLOUCESTERSHIRE
OS 163 037186
8 miles south-east of Cheltenham

St Oswald, Shipton Oliffe

THE SHIPTON VILLAGES, Oliffe and Solers (on the map, but elsewhere 'Sollers' and 'Sollars'), lie just off the A40 trunk road in the winding valley of a headstream which feeds the River Coln. They take their name from a sheep-farm which was once in the ownership of the abbess of nearby Withington, but by the fourteenth century divided between the Oliffe and Solers families. The villages are contiguous, pleasant enough but with some indifferent modern infill, and each has its own manor house, both much altered in the last 100 years. The churches are the focus.

St Oswald, at Shipton Oliffe, stands in a well-tended churchyard against a backdrop of trees, its roof of stone slates graded in the traditional style. It is a small, aisleless church whose chancel accommodates a gentle dip at ground level. At the west gable is a thirteenth-century bellcote which accommodates two bells and has

a pyramid-shaped roof supported by pinnacled buttresses; and on the south side of the chancel is an early Decorated window with two sensitively carved heads and dogtooth moulding.

The church was restored in 1903–4 by H. A. Prothero who unfortunately replaced two of the plain rectangular windows, one on either side, with his larger version to allow more light. Within, he rebuilt the small, low chancel arch. There are lancet windows in the chancel, but elsewhere trefoil is the motif, with a rere-arcade at the east. The canopied piscina would be the treasure, but sadly it is in a poor state of preservation.

St Mary at Shipton Solers is less than half a mile away to the west. It stands above the road in a group of manor house, farm and stables. The church is not unlike St Oswald; a small, appealing, thirteenth-century building with nave and chancel, the latter again lower than the nave; but the bellcote here is nineteenth-century, a rebuild or perhaps imitation of Shipton Oliffe, and not in the same class. The church was well restored in 1929 when a colourful reredos, painted by W. Ellery Anderson, was inserted and the electric light, with pendants of wrought iron, installed. The east window, by Geoffrey Webb, looks less convincing. The church is not often in use and is invariably locked, but the windows are low enough to see through without even standing on tiptoe.

THE WYCHWOOD from which three villages take their title was a huge forest named after the Hwicce, an old English people who inhabited this territory 1,500 years ago. It once covered a wide area between Chipping Norton and Woodstock; now it is reduced in size to about four square miles south-west of Charlbury. Shipton is the largest of the settlements so named, and has a number of old houses grouped around a spacious green with the church of St Mary, down by the River Evenlode, constantly in view. The short Early English tower surmounted by its Perpendicular spire looks well enough, though perhaps a little earthbound; not the most blithe of compositions from the springtime of Gothic.

The Shaven Crown Inn was purpose-built in the fifteenth century, reputedly by the monks of Bruern Abbey two miles to the north. It has an arched carriageway, some nice knobbly textures and a paved courtyard, and it retains many of its medieval windows. To the north a chimney-stack survives, and in the hall off the entrance there is an original timber roof, much restored. All surviving medieval hostelries have to balance retention of atmosphere with the demands of modern ideas of hospitality (to say nothing of planning authorities or fire officers); the Shaven Crown succeeds better than most.

Shipton Court, on a gentle slope to the south-west, dates from 1603 and was one of the grandest Jacobean houses in the county. The west front, facing the road, has eleven bays under five gables, symmetrical and of excellent proportions. The school north of the church is by G. E. Street, an essay in Gothic with extremely sharp gables. Street also provided the church, school and teacher's house at Milton-under-Wychwood, a mile to the west. Taken individually, these buildings are unlikely to be to the taste of many who enjoy the Cotswolds for their traditional architecture, but as a group, correct in stone and textures, they succeed. Commissions of this kind gave Victorian architects perhaps their best opportunity. Tinkering and restoration was the least agreeable part of their trade. Complete and in a group, buildings such as these show Victorian architecture at its best.

Lower Slaughter

The Slaughters

GLOUCESTERSHIRE
3 miles south-west of
Stow-on-the-Wold

Lower Slaughter

OS 163 166226

THESE TWO VILLAGES are among the most famous in the Cotswolds. The name signifies nothing sinister but is derived from the Old English *slohtre*, a slough or muddy place, in this instance the meadows of the River Eye just above its confluence with the Dikler.

LOWER SLAUGHTER is the showpiece, more reticent than some, but still a honeypot to tourists in the summer season. Cottages and gardens are grouped around a green on the north bank of the stream, which is crossed by little stone bridges: the picturesque *par excellence* (**164**). Nearly all the building is of the local stone except for the mill, an early nineteenth-century intrusion in brick, with its huge wheel on show, but silent. Even the local authority's housing, quite properly, has the luxury of Cotswold stone roofs. Private estate developments likewise generally pay respect.

Huge gate-piers in the village street, surmounted by giant finials, announce the Manor House, the work of Valentine Strong, son of Timothy, the founding father of the family who owned the quarries at Little Barrington (q.v.) and Taynton. The date is 1640, although later additions and alterations have somewhat masked his original proportions, now further submerged in a hotel. Architecturally, only the porch gives a hint of former glory. The fenestration is bleak, the stone too 'restored'. Worst of all, the roof is of Welsh slate, and compounds the lumpish look. It is due for renewal. Let it be stone slate, if possible, or an acceptable modern substitute. The stables to the east, of more than a century later, are among the largest and most ambitious in the county.

The church of St Mary, rebuilt in 1867 by Benjamin Ferrey, is uninviting. It has a broach spire topped in fibreglass, and the dark grey pointing makes even the Cotswold stone look unattractive.

Upper Slaughter   OS 163 155233

UPPER SLAUGHTER lies a mile to the north-west. The River Dikler divides the village in two. To the north are cottages backing on to stone-walled upland fields, to the south the church and square, below which a 'no through road' splashes across a ford beside a hump-backed foot-bridge. The church of St Peter is approached through grassy banks and yew. It has an embattled and pinnacled tower, and stone roofs, properly graded but a little mossy. It is in origin a Norman church, whose arcade was taken down in 1822 but sensibly and sensitively put back fifty years later by J. E. K. Cutts. He also opened up the tower arch. There is really little else of interest save the old Perpendicular font, and the mortuary chapel of Francis Witts, rector, lord of the manor, and author of *The Diary of a Cotswold Parson*.* The monument by

---

* A selection, edited and introduced by David Verey, was first published by Alan Sutton of Gloucester in 1978 and has been reprinted a number of times, most recently in 1986.

Francis Niblett of Gloucester is in the style of Pugin, and scholarly in its following of Gothic motif.

The manor was formerly the Wittse's parsonage home, much added to in the mid-nineteenth century, and now the Lords of the Manor Hotel. The (Old) Manor House is quintessential Cotswolds of the Tudor period, a riot of gables, but with a modern gabled extension to the south which detracts from the symmetry; it is sadly never on show to the public. Something of the grandeur can be glimpsed, or snatched on a telephoto lens, through the new iron gate. The core of the Elizabethan building, apart from the dressings, is of rubblestone; the face of the two-storeyed porch, Doric pilasters below and Ionic above, with a frieze and semicircular pediment, is of ashlar, and this greatly enhances the appearance of the house.

Close to the churchyard, and looking into the square, are eight cottages remodelled about 1906 by Sir Edwin Lutyens, who had built Abbotswood three miles to the north-east four years before; they are right in every respect, but then of all the architects who had made a name for themselves since the Industrial Revolution, Lutyens alone understood materials, and above all the spirit of the place.

Somerford Keynes

GLOUCESTERSHIRE
OS 163 016955
5 miles south of Cirencester

THE VILLAGE is four miles from the source of the River Thames, and is now almost an island site as the gravel pits leave large lakes and marinas in their wake. The Manor House, barn, dovecot, former vicarage and church of All Saints make an excellent group. The church has one important feature, a small Saxon doorway (**167**) set in the original north wall of the nave. It was formerly blocked, and only reopened in April 1968. It is an odd shape, tall, cramped and narrow, with primitive carving and cable moulding. Inside the church, above the same door, an oval recess contains (but not *in situ*) a damaged carving of two dragons facing each other. One monster is almost complete; both seem to be biting a ball.

The tower is in the Perpendicular style with a battlement and pinnacles, and was erected in 1710–13, an example, if ever there was, of Gothic survival at its most persistent. There is little else of interest within, save an alabaster monument of 1645 to Robert Straung, reclining on his elbow, in full fig and wig.

South Cerney

GLOUCESTERSHIRE
OS 163 050973
4 miles south of Cirencester

SOUTH CERNEY is on the River Churn. The Cotswold Water Park, part of a sizeable water system created by the extraction of gravel, lies to the south. The village is large and sprawling, but with some good houses, particularly in Church Lane where the Manor House, a trifle plain perhaps, and the Old Vicarage are a pleasing pair. The west end of the village is called Upper Up; Bow Wow, a quiet lane by the church with rarely a dog to be seen, leads between two waterways to a mill. A footpath to the east runs across fields to the towpath of what was once the Thames and Severn

Saxon doorway, All Saints,
Somerford Keynes

Southrop

GLOUCESTERSHIRE
OS 163 203034
4 miles north-east of Fairford

Canal. This is well-watered country, lots of streams and low-lying meadows, horses, Range-Rovers and daffodils. Edward's College, once a home for clergy widows, is well seen from a neighbouring paddock.

The church of All Hallows is large with many features surviving from the Norman, Transitional and Decorated periods. The central tower has lost its spire, removed after it had been struck by lightning in 1857. In the churchyard, just by the south porch, is a tomb-chest, six centuries old, with the shadowy, mossy remains of two effigies. The nave and both aisles are roofed with machine-made pink tiles which are unforgivable, but there is ballflower at the east, and a fine reticulated window at the west. The church underwent a thorough restoration by J. P. St Aubyn in 1862. He added the south aisle, and sited there the original Norman south doorway. It is weather-beaten, richly carved with animals, birds, and several cats. The doorway has no tympanum but in a niche is a sculpture of Christ in Glory and a vestigial Harrowing of Hell.

At the entrance an octagonal font *c.*1350 bids you welcome. St Aubyn copied his south arcade from that of the north, an admirable Early English. Pitch-pine pews predominate; but go to the chancel, for this is where the interest is: a splendid Decorated display, with ballflower at the east window, and ogee arches for the priests' doors and sedilia. The double piscina is exquisitely carved with a vaulted canopy, ivy leaves and what looks like the head of a Chinese mandarin. The oriental mood persists in the painting on wood of a head and foot, part of a twelfth-century rood-screen depicting Christ Crucified, preserved in a glass case on the wall under the tower. It was found in 1912 by Mr Frederick Cox, the village stonemason, when he was repairing the tower. The head is elongated, about six inches long, and leans forward, mustachioed and with eyes closed: a sensitive and intensely felt work.

THE VILLAGE IS SITUATED in flat country on the lower reaches of the River Leach, only four miles or so north of its confluence with the Thames at Lechlade. It has many good houses and farm buildings, including a magnificent stone-roofed barn at the west end of the church, and an old corn mill which was well restored in the 1960s. Ball-finials abound. The Old Vicarage, with its attendant cedar north-west of the church, played an important part in the formative years of the Oxford Movement; John Keble lived there and entertained many who shared his ecclesiastical persuasion.

The church of St Peter stands beside the Manor and farm; the brown-painted window-dressings of the farmhouse are no asset. The church is without aisles or tower, rather impoverished and much restored, and with some indifferent seating. The nave is Norman in origin and a low arch leads to an Early English chancel. The two Elizabethan effigies in the sanctuary are of interest but the most important feature is the Norman font, one of the most richly decorated in the whole of England. It is a circular tub, twenty-eight inches high and of grey limestone, and remarkably well preserved. The proportions are pleasing, and trefoiled arches, with aedicules in the spandrels, frame figures which have easy poses freely carved in deep relief. The decorative border, all of a flutter, has pellet moulding in the interlaced bands.

The figures are sixteen inches high. Moses, represented with horns, faces east holding the Tables of the Law. On his right is the Church Triumphant, with a chalice and pennoned cross, and to the left is Synagogue, blindfold and with a broken staff, on whom Ecclesia turns her back. From south to north, filling the other half of the circumference, are armoured Virtues, with shields of different shapes, triumphing over the Vices. Thus, reading from the south, Pity triumphs over Envy, Temperance over Luxury, Generosity over Avarice, Patience over Anger, Modesty over Excess. Each is named in Latin; the names of the Virtues appear on the arches, and those of the Vices are cut backwards on the panels in mirror-writing – either to emphasize their place in the order of things, or confidently to proclaim the hoped-for outcome in the struggle of Good with Evil.

Connoisseurs of fonts should not miss one of similar age and style at St Peter, Rendcomb, six miles north of Cirencester. It has carvings of eleven of the Apostles, Judas's place being left blank. Patterned grooving and honeysuckle provide the main decorative key. The font at Southrop is certainly the better, but Rendcomb's is accomplished and an interesting comparison.

Standish

GLOUCESTERSHIRE
OS 162 802085
5 miles north-west of Stroud

THE GRAVEYARD OF ST NICHOLAS, below the ridge and on the western extremity of the Cotswolds, has a specially fine collection of large table tombs. This is one of the most atmospheric churchyards in England. The heavy tombs are at all sorts of angles and many are earlier than the eighteenth century; they are of the grey Cotswold stone, and the best are more ambitious than any at Painswick, five miles away in the hills to the east. One dated 1680 has two figures holding hands and wearing full-bottomed periwigs; another of 1718 has on one side a figure of Time with wings, scythe, hour-glass and horns growing from his forehead, and on the other Death, a skeleton with a shroud over its arm, a spade and an arrow, standing on what may be a symbol of eternity, a serpent biting its tail. There is a simple yeoman's stone of 1674, and some fine neo-classical chests. The most memorable, and perhaps one of the earliest in the country, is a large plain tomb of 1653 of a 'yeaman, Samuell Beard'. Bold lettering proclaims he is 'waighting for a joyfull rezurrection'. Two white marble intruders of 1869 and 1972, luckily much lichened, are quite out of place.

The chief feature of the church, built by Benedictine monks, is the Decorated east window, five lights with flowing tracery and two mouchettes. The date is *c.*1310; the glass of 1874 unworthy. The roof of the nave is covered in panelling with no fewer than 180 differently carved bosses. The oak pulpit has inlay and mouldings, and the box pews are plain but spacious, with attractive hinges; they are the work of Anthony Keck, 1764. On the wall is a monument to Sir Henry Winston (died 1609), lord of the manor and ancestor of the Churchill family, to which connection an inscription proudly draws attention. It was restored in 1965 by S. E. Dykes-Bower. A new clergy vestry, sympathetic in design and materials, was added at the south in 1969.

To the north-west of the churchyard is Church House, originally the almonry of the Benedictine priory, buttressed and venerable, but with its uncoursed blocks of stone somewhat over-pointed. The old vicarage, the earliest part of which is 500 years old, is half a mile to the north. Standish Court, approached by an ancient archway to the south-west and now divided into dwellings, is fourteenth-century in origin. Standish is unjustly omitted from most itineraries; but for the churchyard alone it is well worth stretching the western boundaries of the Cotswolds to their limits.

Stanton, Gloucestershire

OF THE SMALLER VILLAGES of the northern range of the Cotswolds, Stanton must be the most beautiful and entire. In comparison with its more famous neighbours at Broadway and Bourton-on-the-Water, it is more withdrawn and thereby more lovable. Even John Wesley, the evangelist, found the village 'dear and delightful'; but then he may have been more affected by the two Kirkham daughters, Sarah and Betsy, who lived here in the 1720s and towards both of whom he was severally attracted, though he never popped the question. Stanton could hardly have looked as spruce then as it does now (**169**).

The stone is predominantly yellow, and the detailing of porches, architraves and dripstones remarkably good, even on humble houses. In part this is the legacy of Sir Philip Scott, an architect who owned the estate from 1906 to 1937 and who set about the restoration of the village with great sympathy. There are three sizeable houses, all of excellent quality: Stanton Court, mainly seventeenth-century and just visible behind a high hedge of yew; the Manor, which in origin is about 100 years earlier, and the Old Manor Farmhouse, its stone chimney-stacks set diagonally at the roof and the date 1618 over a doorway. The chief pleasure, however, is the ensemble of house upon house, some large, some small, all impeccably kept; gables, mullions and dormers, stone walls, stone-tiled roofs, pretty gardens and large forest trees enclosing the view (**171**). This is a village which is too perfect, too neat, too self-conscious for some, but not for me.

The church, dedicated to St Michael, is cruciform, with a west tower and a spire, a tapering octagon which rises from within a solid battlement and parapet with gargoyles at the corners. It composes especially well from the south. The church, although rather dark, is as enjoyable within as without; to the north the three bays of the nave arcade are Norman (one column white, one column yellow), to the south four bays are Perpendicular. The walls are mostly rendered. The main features are a late fourteenth-century pulpit (now no longer used since it was replaced by a Jacobean one, with sounding-board dated 1684), and a Perpendicular carved wooden boss, decorated with a large bird, taken from the aisle roof and now set in the wall of the south aisle. There is some fifteenth-century glass in the east window: figures two feet six inches tall, delicately drawn and coloured mainly in grey-white, yellow and blue. The glass was removed here from Hailes Abbey, four miles to the south, after the Dissolution, and reset by Sir Ninian Comper, together with his own memorial window to those who died in the First World War. Comper and his son Sebastian provided the reredos, rood-screen, altar and communion rails; Sir Ninian designed the organ loft and gallery. For some their work lacks vitality; it is never less than seemly.

A few of the medieval oak benches survive in the nave. The poppy-heads on three of these, presumably frequented by the

Stanton

farming fraternity who brought their animals with them to church, are deeply marked by chains. Georgian gravestones grace a well-tended churchyard. Stanton's broad street climbs the scarp towards Shenberrow Hill. On the way is the Mount Inn, undistinguished architecturally, but offering a roaring fire in winter to fortify the traveller against the cold and wet, and a glorious view in summer across the Vale of Evesham to Bredon Hill and the Malverns beyond.

Stanway
GLOUCESTERSHIRE
OS 150 061323
4 miles north-east of Winchcombe

STANWAY IS SMALL; a few cottages, a large house, a splendid tithe barn, a remarkable gatehouse, and the church of St Peter. It is a memorable sequence, easily missed by the motorist rushing by on the B4077 a few hundred yards to the south.

Like many other villages in the Cotswolds, Stanway had its own quarry, the Jackdaw Quarry, and the quarry at Stumps Cross, just a mile or so up the hill, is working full blast today. The stone for the house and gatehouse came mainly, it appears, from Temple Guit-

ing, four miles to the south; the grey lichen softens the effect of the orange to advantage. The house, built between 1580 and 1640, was altered by the Victorians and later by Detmar Blow. It has charm but is a little sober-sided, and the unbroken fenestration at the south lends a slightly bleak appearance. The cresting on the south is most unusual and may well be unique. The house is now open to the public, and was considered by the late Arthur Negus to be one of the most beautiful romantic houses in England. It is surrounded by a huge wall, contemporary with the original Tudor

Stanway House and St Peter
The Gatehouse, Stanway House ▽
The Courtyard, Stanway House ▷

building (**172**). The gardens are formal, with a canal, a waterfall and some fine trees, and to the east is a pyramid of Vanbrughian proportions, nothing if not an eye-catcher.

The gatehouse is a stylistic amalgam, but picturesque (**173**). It dates from 1630; the bays are Gothic, the gables Dutch, while the chimney-stacks and frame of the gateway are fully Renaissance. Nearly 100 years later, the coat of arms of the Tracy family, the owners, was inserted in the pediment. The arms are framed by an eared architrave, almost square, and surmounted by a miniature triangular pediment. The scallop-shells are heraldic devices; and below the plinths on which the fluted columns stand is a decorative arrangement sometimes known as Jacobean rustication. The other side, facing the house, is quite different with pedimented doorways flanking the arch, and oval windows and an oriel above (**172**). *Mélange*, hybrid, eclectic, call it what you will, but the ashlar and masoncraft are masterly, the carved details impeccable.

The church of St Peter is of interest only as part of the group of gateway and house, but from the tower there is a fine view of the village. Roofs of Stonesfield slates from Oxfordshire abound, similar but smaller and thicker than their famous counterparts from Collyweston in Northamptonshire. Stonesfield slates adorn the roofs of many Oxford colleges and other buildings in west Oxfordshire; they can weigh as much as a ton for every 100 square feet. The last mine closed in 1909, and today the slaters have to look either to the stock of Collywestons or to the reuse of old slates, for they are extremely durable and they will last for centuries.

There are two war memorials by Alexander Fisher with lettering by Eric Gill, one in the porch of the church, and the other a bronze of St George in the village. Sir James Barrie, not inappropriately, designed a large Wendy House cricket pavilion raised on staddle-stones for Countess Wemyss, the political hostess who presided over the local country house party. On the verandah, out of season, in her delightful *Spirit of the Cotswolds** sat Susan Hill, 'smelling the strange smell, an amalgam of whiteing and linseed oil and tea-urn, hearing the ghostly clapping, the creak and clang of tin numbers swinging over on the scoreboard, and the crack of a glorious six high over the roof into the blue Cotswold sky'.

Stow-on-the-Wold
GLOUCESTERSHIRE
OS 163 192258
10 miles north-west of Burford

STOW-ON-THE-WOLD, despite its romantic name, is often for the traveller a general direction on a signpost rather than a place to explore. This scant regard does it less than justice, but standing as it does at the crossing of roads to Worcester, Cheltenham, Gloucester, Bristol, Swindon, Oxford, Banbury and Birmingham, it gets more than its fair share of traffic, and this must diminish its appeal. Yet there is much to enjoy.

The town was founded in the middle of the eleventh century as a commercial venture with the purpose of exploiting this major

* Michael Joseph, 1988.

intersection; the entrepreneur was the abbot of Evesham. Stow then became a thriving market town primarily for sheep, with two annual fairs, and its later prosperity owed much to agriculture and the local trade in boots and shoes. Many of the buildings that survive reflect its economic history and its standing as a small town of regional importance. It is now all part of the antiques road show.

The Market Square, although too full of parked cars, is among the most attractive in the Cotswolds, and retains much of its medieval plan, with narrow streets leading off almost unnoticeably at the corners. St Edward's House, ashlar with a classical façade of Corinthian fluted pilasters under a cornice, is its most distinguished building. There are a number of welcoming hotels and inns, some dating from the sixteenth and seventeenth centuries, although they often underwent a facelift and even drastic remodelling in the centuries that followed. The White Hart (next door to the youth hostel), The Unicorn and The Talbot are all worth a visit, and if this is not enough to quench a thirst, try the Royalist Hotel, formerly The Eagle and Child, at the bottom of Digbeth Street. This comprises two houses which incorporate timber-framing of the sixteenth century and a fine collar-beam roof within.

J. L. Pearson's large house, Quarwood, out on the Fosse Way half a mile to the south, was built in the Gothic style in 1857. It is splendidly sited but hidden by trees, and only the gateposts on the main road testify to its presence. Ten years earlier Pearson had been responsible for the restoration of the parish church of St Edward, although it had previously been rescued from ruin in the 1680s. In origin it is a building of the thirteenth century with rubble for the walls and ashlar for the tower, but the interior is now too much that of a 'town' church – large, rather pretentious, and too heavily pewed to have much soul or to be at all inviting. Naked light bulbs do not help, and the stained glass of 1882, especially in the east and west windows, is not at all to be recommended. The cake shop in the Market Square certainly is.

Sudeley

GLOUCESTERSHIRE
OS 163 033277
1 mile south-east of Winchcombe

SUDELEY CASTLE is strong on history. Queen Elizabeth slept here, Catherine Parr lived here, Sir Thomas Seymour possessed it; and on a fine day, with its mellow ashlar glowing in a declining sun, the architectural appeal of a romantic ruin juxtaposed with house and chapel is irresistible. The castle was built on the profit of the French wars by Ralph Boteler, Admiral of the Fleet, who held the castle from 1398 to 1469, quite a span in those days. His buildings include the gateway, the two towers, Portmare to the west, the Garderobe to the east, and the Great Barn. What looks like a Great Hall turns out to be the Presence Chamber, a truly royal suite of rooms on the first floor with an appropriately grand bay-window. This building came a little later, as did the Dungeon Tower and kitchen.

The chapel, which serves as the parish church of St Mary, was

St Mary, Sudeley

built by Ralph Boteler *c.*1460. It has a Perpendicular exterior, rich with embattled parapets. The church was damaged during the Civil War when the castle, which was used by Prince Rupert as a Royalist headquarters, was besieged and subsequently wrecked by a Parliamentary garrison. Thus the interior of the church is now entirely the work of Sir George Gilbert Scott. The chancel and nave are both under one roof. In 1984 the fifteenth-century oak screen, which marked the divide, was removed to the back. In principle this must be wrong, but then St Mary was no longer a medieval church, and the move perhaps justified. The new arrangement certainly admits more light in what was hitherto a deeply depressing interior, but the alabaster and marble revealed at the east end are of no great beauty. Two little panels of thirteenth-century glass in a window to the north are unfortunately corroded, although the colours – pink, green, yellow, blue, white and red – are attractive.

The interior of the castle has been much altered and is mostly Victorian. The best room is the Library with an early Elizabethan fireplace, not *in situ*, but perhaps originally intended for the gallery. The interest of this house is primarily in the contents, for this is a private museum, though regularly open to the public. There is a formidable collection of paintings, among them works by Rubens, Van Dyck and Constable. There is also a large and well-preserved sixteenth-century Sheldon tapestry with flowers and birds and scenes in medallions, and a French bed with hangings from Aubusson. Some excellent furniture is on show and some autograph letters from celebrities.

Outside, the gardens were laid out at the time of the Victorian restorations, but in the Elizabethan style, with yew hedges and parkland beyond. They are immaculately kept. There is a falconry, an ornamental lake, and peacocks proudly on patrol.

Swell
GLOUCESTERSHIRE
1½ miles west of Stow-on-the-Wold

THIS COUPLE OF SWELLS has nothing to do with the best hotels nor the top manual of that generally most intrusive of church furnishings, the organ; they derive their name from the old English *swelle*, a swelling, used of a hill or ridge, and they are situated in the pleasant valley of the River Dikler, a mile or so from its source.

Upper Swell
OS 163 176269

UPPER SWELL is to the north. The village clusters around the Manor House; it makes a charming scene of lake and bridge set against a gentle hill and forest trees. The Manor has a two-storey Jacobean porch, flamboyant of its kind, with strapwork, Tuscan columns and a coat of arms in the pediment. The porch is of ashlar, while the rest of the front is of rubblestone, as good an illustration of such juxtaposition as at Upper Slaughter (and closer to public view). Even so, inspection is not easy: the house is partially obscured by the churchyard wall. Cottages are grouped picturesquely round a pond and an early nineteenth-century watermill, still with its wheel but regrettably roofed with Welsh slate. A narrow eighteenth-century bridge crosses the river. The church of St Mary is of rubblestone, with some ashlar at the nave, and the south porch has a Norman door with traces of a tympanum. The chancel is Early English, and has a triple rere-arch at the east end, but the Norman chancel arch has been rebuilt. The flagged stone floor greatly enhances the atmosphere of a medieval church.

Lower or Nether Swell
OS 163 176257

IN LOWER OR NETHER SWELL the church of St Mary is now largely Victorian, the work of J. C. Buckler, 1852. The original Norman church, mostly of ashlar, forms the south aisle, and over the south door there is a tympanum with a dove pecking at the branches of a Tree of Life. Inside, the chancel arch of the Norman church has an extraordinary assembly of carvings: fish, hare, stag, salamanders and on the capitals serpents, a dancing woman with a stick, and human heads. The symbolism, if ever there was any cohesive explanation, is elusive, but the figures are no less fun for all that. The church has stained glass and a set of murals by Clayton and Bell to mark the half-century of the Revd David Royce's incumbency. They relate the events of the Passion; the glass is of moderate quality, the paintings preferable, but the scheme as a whole will have its devotees and should be preserved.

[177]

Spa Cottages, Lower Swell

At the village crossroads is a war memorial by Lutyens, one of many that he provided up and down the land in simple and moving good taste. To the north is Abbotswood, a house designed by him in 1901, during his most prolific period, and built of coursed rubble with ashlar dressings. Lutyens also laid out the gardens, occasionally open to the public, making delicious play with water, formality and flowers, and designing gazebos and dovecots to match. A few years later Sir Guy Dawber had his say at Nether Swell Manor. His work, as elsewhere in the Cotswolds, shows care and respect for local materials and traditional style, but for invention and fluency he is not in the same league.

On the busy road to Stow is a row of cottages which has either been inspired by nearby Sezincote or built with some of the left-overs. It marks an attempt to exploit the medicinal properties of a chalybeate spring identified in 1807. Lower Swell never began to rival Cheltenham, but Spa Cottages' fanciful and Hindu-hooded Gothick, all ogee and crinkled, with a parapet of triglyphs, metopes and paterae, not to mention two sweepily-spiky dormers, is a first-rate collector's item.

Swinbrook

OXFORDSHIRE
OS 163 280122
2½ miles east of Burford

SWINBROOK STANDS ABOVE the River Windrush. This is Mitford country, where Nancy pursued her childhood loves and where she and her sister Unity lie buried in the churchyard. For over three centuries the village was to a large extent under the thumb of the Fettiplace family, the last of whom died in 1805; in the same year their great house, reputedly one of the grandest in the

Fettiplace Monuments, St Mary,
Swinbrook

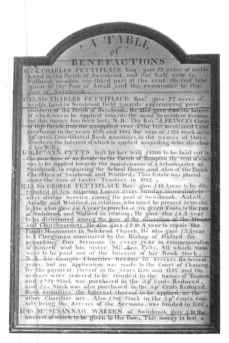

Table of Benefactions, St Mary,
Swinbrook

county, was demolished. No trace or record of this building remains, but in death the family is strongly represented in the church of St Mary just to the north of the site of their home.

The monuments dominate the north wall of the chancel and sanctuary. They are each of three tiers with reclining effigies, one on top of the other, arranged not unlike weary travellers in an old-fashioned second-class railway couchette. The earlier tomb, 1613, looks renewed. Sir Edmund Fettiplace is on the top bunk, and his father and grandfather below, all in armour in which it looks impossible to move, and reclining with some awkwardness on one elbow. The monument is of stone, with a classical surround of fluted columns below a segmental arch flanked by little obelisks, and is probably the work of a local stonemason. The later composition, in the same arrangement but more refined, is dated 1686 and signed by the Oxford sculptor, William Bird. The surround is more delicate, the columns Corinthian, and the occupants more relaxed but still not entirely comfortable. One cannot help but wonder whether, given another chance, they might not all have preferred to travel first class.

The five stalls in the choir come from Burford, and have misericords of exceptional quality. These include a man with a stick, a large and unusual example, and three other single half-length figures. The elbow-rests are particularly effective, a man with arms hanging down, another with a forked beard, and a fish. This admirable woodwork dates from the fifteenth century. The nave is lofty and the east window low, with mostly clear glass; the landscape beyond becomes part of the experience within. The pews are in memory of Lord Redesdale, the Mitfords' father. A table of benefactions (**179**), painted on wood and exquisitely lettered, lists local worthy acts. Sir George Fettiplace intended his beneficiaries to come to church to qualify for their sixpenny loaf, and the provision for his four commemorative sermons each year seems optimistic. Even so, he must have expected the commission to be popular, for the arrangements for settling the arrears are nothing if not businesslike.

Taynton

OXFORDSHIRE
OS 163 233136
1½ miles north-west of Burford

TAYNTON STANDS ON A GENTLE RISE above the valley of the River Windrush. It is the home of the oldest and most famous of Cotswold quarries. The village is a neat collection of cottages and houses, often restored but mostly seventeenth-century, in which gables and mullioned windows play their traditional part. The church of St John the Evangelist overlooks the valley with views down to the willow-banks below. It is approached from the north by a wide path lined with yew. This north side has the showpiece, an aisle with embattled parapet and gargoyles, built *c.*1360 and generously decorated with ballflower and flowing tracery. The south aisle and clerestory were added *c.*1500 and, within, the roof has some excellent wooden bosses carved in various forms – serpent, pomegranate, vine – and adorned with rosettes. The early fifteenth-century octagonal font has the symbols of the Evangelists: a winged man for Matthew, a lion for Mark, for Luke an ox, and an eagle for John. They appear in panels divided by kneeling angels.

The old quarries lie a mile and a half to the north. They were worked by the Saxons and are recorded in Domesday; for the most part they are now a sad but romantic sight, overgrown and marked by trees, although some stone was being extracted until quite recently. These quarries yielded a buff-coloured oolitic limestone capable of a fine ashlar which has played a noble part in our architectural inheritance. Much of the stone went by water to Oxford, and great blocks loaded on carts and dragged by teams of horses were used in the building of Blenheim. For a detailed account of the quality and use of this and other famous limestones quarried along the valley of the Windrush, W. J. Arkell's book *Oxford Stone*,* is indispensable (although long out of print).

Tetbury

GLOUCESTERSHIRE
OS 163 890929
12 miles south-west of Cirencester

FROM NEARLY EVERY DIRECTION, Tetbury announces itself in the distance by the lofty spire of its parish church. It is only two or three miles from the Wiltshire border, marked by the Roman Fosse Way which linked Exeter and Bath to Cirencester and beyond. Until 1964 it was best approached by one of those meandering Cotswold railway branch lines, changing at Kemble on the former Great Western. The middle of the town, where the road from Bath

* Faber, 1947.

Long Street, Tetbury

to Cirencester crosses that from Malmesbury to the north and west, is suitably dominated by the Market House, for this was always a thriving market town for wool and other agricultural produce. The Market House, used probably for weighing wool, was built in 1655 when the town was at the height of its prosperity. It is a large space, seven by three bays in dimension, supported on rather ungainly Tuscan columns. To the south this ground floor has been filled in, but the north remains much as it was with two stone arches, pilasters, cornice and a gabled pediment above. The west front has unfortunately been roughcast. It has a stone roof, a cupola, and best of all a weather-vane sporting a couple of gilded dolphins. It is a building of no great beauty, but a distinctive, somewhat brooding presence at the town centre.

Tetbury is worth a serious perambulation. To the north, Chipping Street leads to an open space which is now, as so often in these small towns, a depository for that unrelenting intruder, the parked car. This was another market, for that is what the word Chipping or Chepying, as in Chipping Campden (q.v.), means. There are some handsome houses, particularly the Priory, a large eighteenth-century building to the west, but to the east, the site of a former Cistercian monastery, a much earlier history is revealed: a twelfth-century window appears between numbers 15 and 17, and two medieval arches hide away in the nearby alley.

The most striking survival is the medieval street (for pedestrians only) known as Chipping Steps (**183**), which descends steeply towards the Avon below. It is paved in rubbly stone throughout; it recalls Vicars' Close in Wells, with the advantage of a sharp descent, though of course without such a perfect assembly of medieval houses. At the bottom is The Croft, one of the best houses in the town, in ashlar with a stylish Regency wrought-iron balcony and a veranda which would not be out of place in Cheltenham. Next door is the no less delightful Croft Cottage (**185**), the house in miniature, likewise ashlar, with bold quoins, segmented windows and keystones. The fenestration is irregular and something of a puzzle, square at ground level and narrow and unaligned on the first floor, but it has a stone-slate roof and presents a compelling focus at the bottom of the Steps.

Long Street (**181**, **184**), which runs west of Market Place, has the best array and variety of houses. The Close, three storeys high and with four gables, is now one of Tetbury's high-class hotels, but until the 1950s it was the most important private residence in town. The garden front to the rear has suffered many alterations, but within, the drawing room has an elegant plaster ceiling and fireplace in the style of Adam. Along the whole street, old gables jostle with Georgian façades, ubiquitous antiques with humbler newsagents and bakery; rubblestone, mullion and transom with urbane ashlar and sash. Sir William Romney's School, a Georgian front with classical porch, is now a surgery (doctors often seem to

Chipping Steps, Tetbury ▷

[182]

Long Street, Tetbury

do themselves well) and number 43 next door, gabled and six-teenth-century in date, has a wrought-iron lamp-bracket over the door. Some of these Georgian fronts surely hide timber-framed structures behind.

Ashlar in Tetbury, as in Malmesbury five miles to the south-east, is more the exception than the rule; on some of the rubblestone houses and cottages, ashlar was considered too expensive even for window-dressings, and a rather mean-looking wood had to suffice. Moreover the rubblestone is not always appealing; it is subject to decay and often looks rather grubby. This explains why here, as in Malmesbury, recourse was too often necessary to rendering – quite a let-down in a limestone town, but, happily, nearly everywhere stone-slate roofs predominate.

All the other main streets are rewarding, and each offers a mixture of date, style and use of stone. Silver Street leads to the Wiltshire bridge, dating from the sixteenth century, and once the county boundary. Church Street drops down towards Bath Bridge, stately and high above a tributary of the Avon. It was built by Thomas Webb in 1774–6, of four arches of coursed rubble, and would have been better still if he could have afforded ashlar.

However short a time a visitor has in Tetbury, the parish church of St Mary should not be missed; it is most original, and worth every effort to find the key. The architect and builder was Francis Hiorn(e) of Warwick, who, writes H. M. Colvin, 'was one of the most accomplished designers of the elegant, decorative Gothic of the late eighteenth century, of which Tetbury church is an excellent example'.* Like his better-known predecessor Francis Smith 'of Warwick' (1672–1738), whose bust by Rysbrack Hiorn left to the

*A Biographical Dictionary of British Architects 1600–1840, John Murray, 1978.

Croft Cottage, Tetbury

Radcliffe Library at Oxford, he served his town as mayor three times. He was working at Tetbury between 1777 and 1781, and built his church on the site of the former medieval church. This exterior with its huge windows is most effective, and the quality of the stone a great attraction.

The interior is wonderfully light, but the plan is freakish: a true *Hallenkirche*, where the aisles and nave are the same height, but with a low-level passage, a kind of enclosed cloister, going nearly the whole way round the church outside the main walls. It is odd, if not unique. The woodwork, including the box pews, is pleasing, and the lacquered candelabra magnificent, but the iron piers (masked with painted wood) are thin and rather spindly. The vault is of plaster. For Olive Cook* it is unacceptably *outré*: 'picturesque preoccupation with scale in its exaggerated height, the exaggerated slenderness of its piers, the exaggerated tallness of the pier bases, and the strange effects of proportion achieved by the placing of the gallery'. *Chacun à son goût.* It is perhaps more curious than

* *English Parish Churches*, Edwin Smith, Olive Cook and Graham Hutton, Thames and Hudson, 1976.

beautiful, but this is a church which wears its Gothic with a smile.

None the less it contains a prize instance of the folly of moving the organ from the west gallery, invariably the best place for it aesthetically, into the body of the building. The gallery has no west window, and now has a blank recess, a void aching to be filled, whereas the organ chamber is an ugly lump in a false chancel at the east end of the south aisle, an eyesore in an otherwise distinguished and singular church. A much-noticed inscription on a wall monument to the east of the south door ends this catalogue of oddities:

> In a vault underneath
> lie several of the Saunderses
> late of this parish: particulars
> the Last Day will disclose.

Tetbury has always been a social centre. There are inns and hotels of top quality. The Talbot Hotel has a piazza-like arcade for frontage, and The White Hart, now renamed The Snooty Fox, was rebuilt in the nineteenth century and once kept a ballroom for the Beaufort Hunt. More recently no fewer than three royals have made country homes near the town, to the advantage of the tourist trade, and no doubt also of the estate agents. There may be prettier towns in the Cotswolds; but with its variety and its unusual church, Tetbury has a special identity.

Toddington

GLOUCESTERSHIRE
OS 150 035331
4 miles north of Winchcombe

TODDINGTON IS JUST BELOW the Cotswold scarp; not *in* the Cotswolds, for the pedantic, but too close to be resisted. In the park, full of forest trees and grazing sheep, the infant River Isbourne has been widened and landscaped; but its manor house and church are what make Toddington memorable.

In 1798 Henrietta, daughter and heiress of the last Viscount Tracy, whose arms appear on the gatehouse at Stanway, married Charles Hanbury, son of a wealthy ironworks owner in Pontypool. He added a hyphen and Tracy to his name, entered public life, and became Member of Parliament for Tewkesbury in 1807. In 1835, as chairman of the commissioners appointed to judge designs for the new Houses of Parliament, he stood by the choice of Charles Barry. Hanbury-Tracy already had credentials of his own as an architect: in 1819 he had demolished the seventeenth-century manor here at Toddington, leaving only the gatehouse ruins to the west of the church (**188**), and supplied his own Gothic designs for the rebuilding which took place to the north between 1820 and 1835 (**187**). His creation can undoubtedly stand comparison with Barry's masterpiece at Westminster.

The principal front faces north and is almost symmetrical. It is an ornate yet dignified building with a large central tower which forms both the pivot and the focus of the composition. The house is constructed entirely of yellow-brown stone, the detailing of which, even when seen at a distance from the field to the north of the church, remains crisp and clear. Neither the skyline nor the

Toddington Manor

south front is symmetrical. Charles Hanbury-Tracy, later Baron Sudeley, had been educated at Christ Church, Oxford. His inspiration drew on examples of Gothic published by the elder Pugin, such as Magdalen College tower, which provided the model at Toddington, but in other respects his house recalls Thomas Rickman's court at St John's College, Cambridge. It is, by any account, picturesque.

If Toddington Manor is unique, the church of St Andrew is surprising. It is one of the finest Victorian churches in the country. The architect is G. E. Street, too often prone to ruin and over-restore the medieval. His church, 1873–9, replaced an earlier rebuilding of 1723. It is built of an orange-yellow stone, perhaps from Guiting, with a tall broach spire placed characteristically and asymmetrically above the south transept. This church has little to do with the Gloucestershire countryside, but the interior reveals Street at his most masterful. It is wide and lofty; sumptuous, yet in no respect vulgar, and faced with a white ashlar. All the eastern part of the church, which is in the early Decorated style, is vaulted.

The nave has a bold hammerbeam roof, and much Purbeck marble and polished granite is on show. The west window provides a theatrical backdrop to an arcade which screens the last bay of the nave. The chancel has a large Decorated window glazed by Clayton and Bell, and for the paving pinkish marble is used in conjunction with plain to telling effect. On the north is a large vaulted mortuary chapel, containing the tomb of the first Lord Sudeley and his wife. It is made of marble – Sicilian for the steps, Carrara for the figures –

and the church seems virtually to have been built around this memorial. Chairs, nearly always preferable unless the pews are Georgian or medieval, provide the seating.

There is a sting in the tail. Below the north gables is a frighteningly realistic gargoyle, a ferocious and scaly dragon spreading his wings to carry off an anguished hostage whose hair stands on end. Fear not, this monster is there to spout nothing more harmful than rainwater.

◁ Old Manor Gatehouse (ruin)
and St Andrew, Toddington
Gargoyle, St Andrew, Toddington

Upton House
WARWICKSHIRE
OS 151 370457
7 miles north-west of Banbury

THE VILLAGE OF UPTON disappeared in the late Middle Ages. The house stands alone just south of the Edge Hill quarries, which yield a Liassic ironstone close in colour and texture to the stone (now no longer worked) from Hornton, two miles to the east across the Oxfordshire border. There is a stately formal approach through an avenue of pines which reveals a north front of nine bays with two slightly projecting wings and a rainwater head dated 1695. The Hornton stone is a golden yellowy-brown, with a lighter stone in the centre at the top, and the house has a stone roof punctuated by dormers. There is a jaunty baroque flourish over the central doorway which anticipates a sprightly welcome; it is apparently the work of Morley Horder who was involved in alterations and additions here in 1927–8. He did a good job, and restored something of the symmetry of the seventeenth-century building. The garden front hides behind an excess of wistaria.

The interior is opulent in both décor and furnishing; architecturally it is almost entirely of this century. The Entrance Hall is of exquisitely ashlared stone, pale gold in colour. Brussels tapestries cover the walls. The oak staircase has balusters (some old, some copied) springing as if from leaves. The chief interest, however, is the assembly of pictures and porcelain, the legacy of Lord Bearsted, one of the most distinguished collectors of his time, who gave it along with the house to the National Trust. There are early Flemish paintings by Brueghel, Memling and van der Weyden, and among the other pictures a panel by El Greco (a model for his altarpiece in Toledo Cathedral), a Stubbs and a Hogarth. The porcelain collection – Sèvres, Meissen as well as Derby and Worcester – must be extraordinarily precious but too ornate to be to everybody's taste.

The gardens to the south of the house have an exhilarating sweep of lawn terminated by a steep drop to a broad canal. To the west is another pool and a water garden, and a gardener's cottage in red brick with pedimented dormers. The temple at Temple Pool, half a mile to the south of the house, is attributed to Sanderson Miller who lived nearby at Radway.

Westwell

OXFORDSHIRE
OS 163 223100
2½ miles south-west of Burford

WESTWELL IS IDYLLIC. Surely nothing could be more pleasurable than to sit on the green by the duck-pond in spring sunshine surrounded by such a lovely sight. An ensemble of cottages, church, rectory, manor house and barns, all in the local stone with steeply pitched roofs, make this a most rewarding village which retains an uncultivated charm (**192, 193**).

The church of St Mary is Norman, nestling within a well-kept churchyard amid some tomb-chests with fine, if fading, carved lettering. It is small, but was enlarged by one bay to the west in a restoration of 1869. At that time a wooden bellcote over a substructure of lead was added. A little porch at the south protects a Norman doorway with zigzag and scalloped capitals and a sundial carved in the tympanum above. Within, under a plain roof of original timbers, interest focuses on two monuments. There is an unusually fine Jacobean male effigy of a former rector, Richard Thornton, 1599–1614, recumbent in a ruff and long robe. On the wall is a monument dated 1657, the period of the Commonwealth. It is to Charles Trinder and his wife, carved in stone with no fewer than fourteen children all kneeling before a cross, a work of no great sophistication but inventive and appealing.

Sir Stuart Holland bought the manor in 1912, and he and Lord Redesdale did much to undo the 1869 restoration, reflooring the church with Cotswold flags and removing polychrome tiles. They are suitably commemorated in two finely lettered tablets in the chancel. From the church a path leads to the former Rectory, a splendid seventeenth-century house, five bays of two storeys, handsome in its ashlar with large mullioned and transomed windows under a modillion cornice at the eaves. The setting is delightful, although creeper is in danger of encroaching too far on this excellent front. The Manor House, south of the church, retires behind high trees. Its entrance is marked by a gateway with sphinxes carved on the gateposts.

A war memorial on the green incorporates a brass numeral from the shattered Cloth Hall at Ypres. An archway of clipped privet adorns a cottage porch; Irish yews stand sentinel. Roses abound, moorhens paddle the pond where yellow irises grow wild.

Winchcombe

GLOUCESTERSHIRE
OS 163 023282
7 miles north-east of Cheltenham

DURING THE PERIOD between Cirencester's abandonment by the Romans and its revival in the Middle Ages, Winchcombe became the most important town in the Cotswolds. Nowadays it is somewhat neglected. Tourists rush through between Cheltenham and Stratford-on-Avon, or hurry on to the attractions of Sudeley Castle nearby. The town deserves much closer attention. The streets show a variety of buildings in stone, wood and plaster, and Winchcombe's historical importance goes back well before the Conquest.

The kings of Mercia had a residence here, and one of them, Kenwulf, founded a monastery in 798. His son Kenelm was murdered, it was alleged, by an ambitious sister who aimed to put a lover on the throne. A white dove flew off with a note to tell the pope; a white cow led the search for the young king's headless body, which was found and brought to Winchcombe. On seeing it, the wicked sister was struck blind by divine vengeance, and other miracles followed. It was an unlikely tale, invented by an eleventh-century monk and given credibility in the retelling by William of Malmesbury a century later. Later investigations showed the story to be suspect: Kenelm died before his father (who was succeeded by his brother).

The tomb, however, became an important shrine of pilgrimage, and a large Benedictine abbey, among the grandest and wealthiest of Anglo-Saxon England, grew up around it on a site north-east of the present parish church. The abbey was completely destroyed at

Westwell, Oxfordshire

the Dissolution by Lord Seymour of Sudeley, who in 1547 married Henry VIII's widow, Catherine Parr. Not a stone stands, though no doubt many were reused in and around the town. Two buildings occupy the site: one (much restored) claiming to be the former malt-house, and another, an eighteenth-century bow-fronted house, the former Abbey Hotel, now in private hands.

The parish church was built between 1456 and 1474. The abbey financed the chancel and the parishioners the nave, helped by Sir Ralph Boteler, the builder of Sudeley Castle. The chancel was heightened in 1690 and the whole church restored by John Drayton Wyatt, a partner of Sir George Gilbert Scott, in 1872. It is one of the largest of the Cotswold wool churches yet one of the least elaborate. The outside holds much promise. The browny-grey stone is welcoming, and the south side of the tower, stately but not particularly lofty, is a fine example of medieval ashlar. The tower has eight pinnacles, and from the centre rises a huge gilded weathercock which was translated from St Mary Redcliffe in Bristol at the time of Wyatt's restoration. The tower, aisles, nave and south porch are all enlivened with embattled parapets and pinnacles, and there is a series of about forty grotesques – not, strictly speaking, gargoyles (because no water-channels run through them), but fashioned in the same way. They are an extraordinary bunch, a little weathered, sometimes macabre, but often amusing: a jolly jester with moustache, a leering, jeering

Westwell, Oxfordshire

demon, a monstrous pig, terrifying apes, and the mitred abbot himself, a trifle bemused to find himself in such company.

The interior is spacious, wide but dull. There is no chancel arch, the piers are plain and octagonal, and the clerestory, an almost continuous row of flat-headed windows, lacks interest. The church is much Victorianized. The east window, depicting Christ walking on the water beside a boat full of his disciples, is a pictorial *tour de force*, but an artistic catastrophe. The altar cloth, made out of priests' copes dating from the 1380s and now on show in a frame in the north aisle, is historically precious but has faded to a shadow of its former self. The font canopy of 1634 is original and there are a number of interesting monuments: one, on the north wall of the sanctuary and dated 1636, is of a kneeling judge Thomas Williams of Corndean. It has paint on stone, but is more remarkable for a humility not normally associated with judges. Space is left for his wife, but she married another and is buried elsewhere.

Immediately south-west of the church is the town's most distinguished building, Jacobean House (**194**), a wool merchant's residence dating from the seventeenth century, with two gables, ball finials and a handsome porch. Round the back, on the west side, is an outside staircase. The front composes well, complete with mullioned and transomed windows, but the appearance is marred by an ugly gutter-pipe. Close by to the south are the Chandos Almshouses, which were built in 1573 but lost some of

Jacobean House, Winchcombe

their character in the Victorian reordering of 1841. At Dent's Terrace, Sir George Gilbert Scott built the Sudeley Almshouses of 1865. They suit the location well but are somewhat contrived in their use of different-coloured stones. Polychrome has no place in the Cotswolds. Scott also designed the School House, built as a school to the west of the church in 1868.

Winchcombe has a fair sprinkling of inns and pubs of character. The High Street has the George Hotel, now sadly vacant and ripe for development. It was an inn for pilgrims built round a courtyard and much altered over the centuries, but bears the carved initials of a former abbot, Richard Kidderminster, in the spandrels of the entrance. The White Lion in North Street will whet an appetite, and the Old Corner Cupboard Inn, intriguing both in name and appearance, stands towards the west end of the town in Gloucester Street, lined with many interesting houses ranging from the sixteenth to the nineteenth century.

At the bottom of Castle Street is the Great House, dignified and square, if a little dowdy, mullioned and transomed, and ashlared with a modillion eaves cornice. It has a hipped roof, and the whole of the Winchcombe roofscape is worth careful scrutiny. Like Stamford in Lincolnshire, another limestone town, Winchcombe has a number of mansard roofs – roofs with two pitches on each side of the ridge, the lower one steeper than the upper. The effect is to produce more standing room in the attic, but with the more recent mansard roofs the lower slope is all too often well-nigh vertical and the dormer windows extravagantly large, which is unsightly. Fortunately, except in the eastern counties of England, especially Lincolnshire and the Fens, the style has never been popular. At Winchcombe, mansard roofs by no means dominate, but they consort oddly with gable and traditional pitch, and are too often clad in slate, unsuitable in any limestone town. Winchcombe must look to the rooftops.

Windrush

GLOUCESTERSHIRE
OS 163 193130
5 miles west of Burford

Ram's head corbel, St Peter, Windrush

WINDRUSH stands roughly midway along the course of the little river whose name it bears. The river flows to join the Thames at Newbridge, in truth quite an old bridge (a mere 500 years), ten miles south-west of Oxford. No name more perfectly captures the spirit and tranquillity of the Cotswolds than Windrush, and no author has written more poetically of the pastoral character of this scene than H. J. Massingham: 'lilies of the valley appear in spring to charm venerable oaks . . . and snowdrops flow in cascades down the banks towards the guelder-roses and willows that edge the stream.'* Fifty years on, little has changed.

The valley is just below the ridge that carries the A40 trunk road. Windrush Mill, a seventeenth-century corn mill, is down by the river to the east: a romantic, rubbly, rustic stone building astride the stream, fringed by trees and rushes. This is perfect harmony. Two village streets spread up the hill in arrowhead formation to reach the church which forms the apex. The green is surrounded by attractive stone cottages and houses. Windrush had its own quarry where the stone was in part mined; building material was readily available and relatively cheap.

The church of St Peter was zealously restored by Henry Woodyer in 1876. Originally it was a Norman church of c.1170 with some Perpendicular additions, notably in the south aisle, the transept and the tower. The south door (**196**) is famous and has a double row of beakheads; despite some staining and an unsatisfactory makeshift porch, this menacing array is in a good state of repair. In a county rich in Romanesque carving, and not forgetting Elkstone and Quenington, Windrush has some of the finest.

In 1839, the Royal Commission (under the chairmanship of Charles Hanbury-Tracy, architect of Toddington Manor q.v.) which was considering the choice of stone for Barry's new Houses of Parliament was much impressed by the perfect condition of this church. It is a great pity Henry Woodyer saw it differently thirty-five years later. Nevertheless the chancel and the arch, with its quaintly splayed Norman jambs, and the aisle arcade are all original and the masonry fine. On the north side of this arcade is a corbel carved in the shape of a ram's head, with Ionic-looking horns. A similar motif appears in the churchyard on one of the baroque table

* *Cotswold Country*, Batsford, 1937.

tombs just outside the south door. In the days of the flourishing wool trade, these people clearly understood that even beyond the grave, their prestige rested on the backs of sheep.

Winson
GLOUCESTERSHIRE
OS 163 092087
2½ miles north-west of Bibury

WINSON IS SMALL and little known, situated on a secluded stretch of the River Coln between the Fosse Way and the road from Cirencester to Burford. There are some splendid barns, the Manor Farm dated 1729, and, in pride of place, just to the north-east of the church, Winson Manor itself, reminiscent of the style of James Gibbs. The ashlar is excellent, and the detailing most accomplished, with architraves, a modillion cornice, pediment and *œil-de-bœuf*. The house is most truly Gibbs at its 'Gibbs surrounds', a motif which consists of alternate larger and smaller blocks of stone set like quoins round doors and windows. They are to be seen here at the ground floor and at the doorway. At the back, stone mullions in the windows indicate that this was an earlier building remodelled in the eighteenth century.

The little church of St Michael is Norman; it has no tower but just a belfry, added in the nineteenth century. The masonry is faultless. The steeply sloping churchyard abounds in table tombs, overgrown by moss and ivy.

Withington
GLOUCESTERSHIRE
OS 163 032156
3 miles south of Andoversford

THE VILLAGE STANDS on either side of the River Coln at the end of a two-mile straight stretch of road leading towards Cheltenham. It was once served by the railway, a minor line which provided an enjoyable excursion along the valley of the river from Andoversford before swinging south to Cirencester. Withington has a long history. In the tenth century, in an early flurry of sex-equality enterprise culture, the abbess was a formidable land-lady who controlled the neighbouring Shiptons, Oliffe and Solers.

The church of St Michael stands on high ground. The central tower is large and, despite its ogee-arched bell openings, bleak in appearance; the pinnacles are tall but too thin and only mark the corners, leaving the crown a little meagre in appearance. The church is Perpendicular, and would be cruciform if it did not lack a north transept. Cobbett called it 'a small cathedral'. It has original Norman building, from which a corbel table was reused at the chancel. The interior was poorly treated in the over-restoration of 1872 by David Brandon, who had also turned his hand to additions at the Rectory and built a new school in the 1850s. The east window in the south chapel is by Sir Ninian Comper, 1949; his work is admired by many but is sometimes feeble in portraiture and anaemic in colour. The monument at the back of the church to Sir John Howe and his wife, portrayed with their eight children, is strong on clothes and fashion; it is by Edward Marshall and dated 1651. Space is provided to record the death of each child, indicating either infantile morbidity or parental preoccupation with life's brief portion. Skulls are a prominent motif; alas! poor Yorick.

◁ South door, St Peter, Windrush

The Old Rectory, close by the church to the east, is huge. Gabled either side and symmetrical in the elevation to the south, it has Tudor origins but was given a formidable face-lift in the eighteenth century. It composes well with the church, seen across water from the south-east when the trees are not in leaf. The Manor House likewise had Georgian alterations, but its mullions and transoms and Jacobean detailing place it less equivocally in the earlier period. The dovecot, gabled, lanterned and full of bird-holes, is one of the best. Corner House incorporates a medieval hall, as does Halewell Close, once in the ownership of the bishops of Worcester. Court House is dated 1753, classical, ashlared, and with a parapet. The medieval Mill Inn and House, a charming duo down by the river, were rebuilt *c*.1960 making use of stone from Northleach Prison.

A mile to the east at Cassey Compton is the Howe family mansion, low-lying in a perfect setting with views across to Chedworth Woods. Only the centre and west wing of the late seventeenth-century house now survive, but they still make a fine group, isolated amongst the fields and trees. In such surroundings, the pylons that stride along the horizon are even less forgivable than usual.

Witney
OXFORDSHIRE
OS 164 356093
10 miles west of Oxford

WITNEY MEANS BLANKETS. Bridge Street, the route from Oxford across the River Windrush, tells the story; long, gaunt Victorian stone buildings, blackened by grime and traffic, bear witness to the town's industrial past. Witney is one of Oxfordshire's oldest recorded towns. From the Middle Ages its prosperity depended on wool, and the town profited handsomely from its readily available water power and its strategic position on the route (now the A40) to London, giving access to markets far and wide. Even in the nineteenth century, when trade mostly shifted to the industrialized north, Witney managed to modernize and survive. This was largely due to the concentration of the manufacture in the hands of two or three local families, notably the Early family who had started business in the town in the seventeenth century.

It was John Early who, in 1818, shortly after the fly-shuttle had been developed in the north, visited Rochdale and ordered spinning machines not only for his own enterprise but for others in the town. Later the railway (now long disappeared), brought cheap coal, and the looms were powered by steam. What remains of Early's Blanket Mills is tucked away in Mill Street. Smith's Blanket Mills, a range built *c*.1900, stand in Bridge Street with workers' cottages of earlier date and the mill-owner's house – Georgian, rendered, shabby but with a sensational fanlight. Most of these industrial antiquities are now submerged in the new trading estate, appropriately located, but unsightly and characterless. Witney's blankets scarcely survived the Second World War; foreign competition, the advent of synthetics, the drift of labour to the machine-tool and car industries all took their toll. Yet

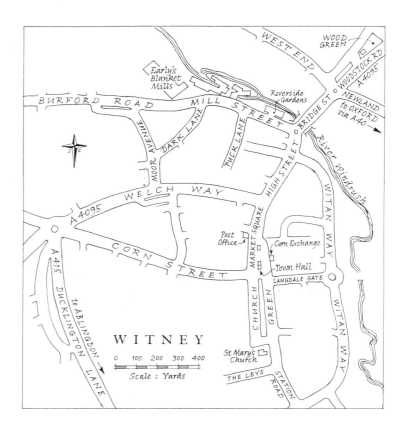

the spirit of six centuries of the woollen industry lives on.

Staple Hall, now a private nursing home in Bridge Street, looks sixteenth-century but goes back much earlier. It has a rather dowdy stuccoed front under two gables with sash windows, double-glazed against persistent traffic noise. In the High Street is the Blanket Hall, a rural baroque of 1721, built for the weighing and measuring of blankets. It has an arched entrance, and at the first storey three long sashed windows on a narrow front below a pediment with a handsome clock. Above is a weather-vane and an odd little cupola behind which lurks a bell turret.

The historic part of Witney is one long street, about three-quarters of a mile long, with a single axis of buildings running from Bridge Street south to the High Street and Market Place. Here at the heart of the town stand the eighteenth-century Town Hall and the Butter Cross (**200**), steep-roofed and dating from around 1600, with a clock turret dated 1683. It has four gables infilled with ugly cement and supported by a central pillar and twelve others of roughish stone. It is picturesque, but further to the south is Witney's single most attractive feature, Church Green, a long open expanse of grass leading up to the parish church of St Mary.

The houses are mainly Georgian and Victorian, but on the east side is The Hermitage (**201**), one of the two dwellings incorporating sixteenth-century work which were reputedly plague retreat

Butter Cross and Town Hall,
Witney

The Hermitage, Witney ▷

houses for Oxford colleges. These houses compose as a group
better than they withstand individual architectural scrutiny. The
best house on the east is St Mary's, near the church (though it hides
behind an efflorescent creeper), and to the west, number 20, which
has five bays with a parapet and a Venetian window.

Nearby is the Grammar School, set back from the road and once
approached by an avenue of ancient elms, which were swept away
in the devastating disease of the 1970s. The replanting is laudable.
This proud school, founded in 1660 by Henry Box whose name it
still bears, is a building of one storey rendered and painted, but
with stone dressings, and with two taller projecting side-wings and
high chimneys. It has seen better days. Some of the modern
additions are purposeful and inoffensive, although concrete and
render are too often on show. The best designs are by A. E. Smith,
a sensitive county architect who did much good work of this kind.

Church Green is an ideal setting for the church (**202**), which
stands on a slight slope commanding the town. Norman in origin,
it was almost entirely rebuilt in the thirteenth century with transepts which have west aisles, and a central tower with corner
pinnacles and an octagonal spire. It is similar in design to the
cathedral at Christ Church, Oxford; above the lucarne it lacks spire
lights and is neither lofty nor especially graceful, but it is decidedly
striking.

St Mary, Witney

The north side is the 'show' front to the town, and therefore the grander and more interesting. In the fourteenth century the north transept acquired a series of chantry chapels in lavish style with diagonal buttresses, niches for images under canopies, a doorway with ogee head, finial and much ballflower. The *pièce de résistance* is a superb Decorated window of seven lights with flowing tracery. The north porch incorporates an upper room whose cornice has a deliciously amusing gargoyle: a wide-eyed head with Dumbo ears (or are they errant wings), paws apart, who looks as if he is in full flood addressing a conference.

At the west end there is a fine Perpendicular window of five lights, and windows of this period also appear at the west end of both aisles. At about the same time the south transept was enlarged and remodelled, the clerestory added, and a parapet built to gird the whole church. The new arrangements at the south-east entrance, with a bleak white infill above a sheet-glass hotel-like entrance door, are the only blot on this fine exterior.

After all this enjoyable display, the interior is disappointing, although much of the quality of the stone is good and the decorative and tracery work on the windows can be appreciated as well within as without. There is a poor reredos, too small for a building of this scale, and a much more dignified high altar is now in place at the crossing under the tower. Regrettably, there is a plethora of ungainly pews. The heavy hand of G. E. Street and the glass of Clayton and Bell has destroyed much of the atmosphere promised by the exterior.

Already in the seventeenth century over 3,000 townspeople were employed in the spinning and weaving of cloth, and until the First World War nearly everyone would have been involved in the industry. A number of smaller, earlier houses can be seen in Westend (Charlbury Road), a street which with some attention could be the most rewarding in town. At Wood Green nearby, close to the river and the mills, some stylish houses were established in the Georgian period with the customary embellishments of doorcases, hoods and fanlights, grouped with humbler cottages and their own church around a small green. Bath House and the Post Office, a little earlier (*c*.1725–50), in the High Street are perhaps grander although both lack the dignity of glazing bars.

Infill housing and westward expansion to accommodate an increased population came in the 1960s – a bad time for domestic building, and however vital socially, architecturally the less said the better. The return to the vernacular in the Woodgate shopping centre, while no doubt sweeping away any amount of old building, is inoffensive. Stylistically it is eclecticism run riot. It has the lot: gables, arcades, domed glass, a spirelet, clock, lancet and oriels – the whole hosier's shop. The cladding, redeemingly, is rubble-stone, and the roofs are right in colour; only the rattle of the supermarket trolleys disturbs the peaceful precinct.

Woodchester
GLOUCESTERSHIRE
OS 162 840027
2 miles south of Stroud

WOODCHESTER, once a centre of the cloth industry, straggles up the slopes and valley between Nailsworth and Stroud. Most of the village is strung out along a road on the side of the hill, an older route to Stroud than the one in the valley, and there are cottages, pubs and a Baptist chapel dated 1825.

Twenty years later, Catholicism put in a strong appearance, largely through the influence of William Leigh who had bought the large estate at Woodchester Park and was a recent convert to the faith. Pugin was always his preferred architect, but he could never nail him down. For his Dominican priory, 1846–9 (now razed to the ground, a sad and empty plot of the remaining church), and the Franciscan convent 1861–9, he had to be content with Charles Francis Hansom, a younger brother of Joseph Aloysius, both of whose names crop up frequently in connection with Catholic architecture up and down the country.

About the same time, the Anglicans abandoned their Norman church of St Mary and commissioned a new building from S. S. Teulon – always an architect of interest, but rarely of sensitivity. To the north is the romantic ruin of the old church, set amongst yews and tomb-chests, and the site of a Roman villa c.AD 300. This had been known since 1695 when Bishop Gibson wrote an appendage to the *Camden Britannia*; the floor was first uncovered by Edmund Browne in 1712 but more completely by Daniel Lysons between 1793 and 1797. It has been damaged by grave-diggers over the years and is now covered by turf. It is about 47 feet square, looks rather like a bowling green and was last exposed in the 1970s. The mosaic is a representation of the Orpheus myth and is one of the finest examples of Roman mosaic work north of the Alps. It is clearly only the tip of an iceberg, for this villa of about sixty rooms is on a more extensive scale than that at Chedworth, but because of its delicate state is left covered and only unearthed to view once in a decade. Two brothers, Bob and Charles Woodward, were so captivated by the mosaic that, working from an exact photographic record, they made a replica in five colours. It is meticulously executed in a million and a half tesserae of limestone from the local quarries and a pinky sandstone from the Forest of Dean. This mosaic is an extraordinary labour of love, once on show in Wotton-under-Edge, but now seeking a more permanent home under the aegis of the Stroud District Council.

William Leigh manifested his energies no less at Woodchester Park. He began by demolishing an earlier house, said by Pugin to be in an irredeemable condition, and from him he commissioned another. As at the priory, Pugin withdrew fearing lack of money to complete the enterprise, and his place was taken by Benjamin Bucknall, an enthusiastic follower, friend and translator of Viollet-le-Duc, the French Gothicist and architectural theorist. The mansion, set in extensive parkland two and a half miles to the west, was never finished. The situation is up a long narrow valley with conifer plantations too close for comfort. The house is built of a fine buff-coloured limestone, and the south front, in the style of the seventeenth century and almost symmetrical, is particularly effective.

The guttering and rainwater pipes, and even the bath (which must have made for Spartan ablutions), are of stone, and there are some marvellous gargoyles of foxes and falcons. The chapel, redolent of incense, has a beautiful vault and a huge 'Decorated' east window and a rose at the west. The finished drawing-room has a lierne vault, but other rooms remain uncompleted. The tower, dated 1858, is something of an encumbrance. It is sad and incongruous to see this important part of our Victorian heritage in its present derelict state. The local council has recently acquired the property and has laudably started work on conservation. A keen preservation group is taking a close interest, and, together with the Council, is looking for a purchaser who would make appropriate use of the site and undertake more systematic restoration.

Wotton-under-Edge

GLOUCESTERSHIRE
OS 162 761934
12 miles west of Tetbury

WOTTON-UNDER-EDGE has a dramatic setting, cut into a valley just below the Cotswold scarp overlooking the Vale of Berkeley. The main street, Long Street, makes a steep ascent with a bustle of shops and houses, the best of which date from the seventeenth and eighteenth centuries when the prosperity of the town was at its height. One whole room from number 31 was sold complete to the Victoria and Albert Museum in 1924. There was a market here in the twelfth century, and the town enjoyed the patronage of the Berkeley family whose castle guarded the Severn ten miles to the north-west. One of their ladies, Katherine, founded a grammar school, one of the oldest in the county, in 1384; its spirit survives, though perhaps somewhat changed in tradition and style, in a building of 1726 in Gloucester Street. It is built of ashlar with sash windows, segmental and moulded architraves, solid but somewhat uninspiring.

Wotton has always looked after its elderly, and there are no fewer than four special provisions. In Culverhay, Miss Ann Bearpacker's Almshouses, a benefaction dating from the accession of Queen Victoria, are Elizabethan in style. In Church Street there are Dawes Hospital of 1720, the General Hospital (most sensitively refurbished 1952–4, preserving both atmosphere and the character of the building), and best of all Hugh Perry's Almshouses. These date from the middle of the seventeenth century; the stone, stripped of its former plaster, is somewhat rubbly and unevenly coursed, particularly in the six gables, and could do with some cleaning, but this charming building breathes tranquillity. In the middle rises a domed wooden cupola, and an alley leads directly off the street to an inner courtyard containing the chapel, collegiate in miniature and atmosphere.

The town has had some colourful residents. The religious attitudes of Isaac Pitman, inventor of shorthand, provoked displeasure, and he was told he would be 'hunted out of the town like a mad dog'. More Adey, a wildly eccentric friend of Oscar Wilde, affected to be Squire of Wotton and spent much of his life hunting for treasure in Under the Hill House.

The parish church of St Mary the Virgin is to the north-east. It has a well-proportioned tower, Decorated in the lower reaches and Perpendicular above. The stone is grey and a little dour, the detailing bleak, and the bell-ringers' windows are wholly blocked. The parapet is relieved by panelling and delicate finials at the corners. The interior is wide and light, and full of monuments of varying quality. The brasses of Thomas Berkeley and his wife Margaret are the most important and quite beautiful. They are said to date from *c.*1390, which would make them among the earliest in the county. In the north aisle is stained glass, a feeble affair by Hardman, who had the temerity to copy figures by Joshua Reynolds.

This interior reveals the hand of three extraordinary incumbents, inventive, enthusiastic, energetic, but not always men of much taste. First came William Tattersall, who inserted the plaster ceilings about 1800 – Gothic revival in style, but a poor substitute for a roof of wood or stone. The architect was Nathaniel Dyer and the plasterer John Pike. He also bought the organ from St Martin-in-the-Fields in London. It had been given by George I, built by Christopher Schrider, and reputedly played by Handel. Next came Benjamin Perkins, who was vicar from 1829–81; he set about the church with a will when congregations were expanding, and took down the chancel arch and screens, built two more bays to the arcades, raised the chancel roof to the height of the nave, and put in new clerestory windows and another window over the sanctuary arch. He also destroyed the three-decker pulpit, and probably the desk and font as well. Lastly there was Henry Sewell; he removed the galleries erected by his Gothicist predecessor Tattersall and in so doing moved the organ, fittingly sited in the west gallery, to its present position in the transept. He also undid some of Perkins's 'improvements', by restoring the chancel as a choir and raising the floor level. He went on to install the choir screen and wrought-iron pulpit and reading-desk. Nowadays enthusiastic clerics and parochial church councils are restrained in their artistic invention by diocesan advisory committees and, it must be said, by paucity of cash. It is no bad thing.

Glossary

AISLE: division of a church at the side, parallel to the nave, and separated by piers, pillars, columns or an arcade.

AMBULATORY: a processional aisle closing a sanctuary or an apse.

ANNULET: a ring round a pier or shaft.

APSE: a semi-circular or polygonal end to a church or chapel.

ARCADE: a range of arches resting on piers or columns; a 'blind arcade' is an arcade attached to a wall.

ARCHITRAVE: 1. The lowest of the three divisions of the classical entablature, below the frieze and cornice. 2. The moulded frame surrounding a door or window.

ASHLAR: masonry of hewn or sawn stone, in blocks which are usually large but often quite thin, carefully squared and finely jointed in level courses.

BALLFLOWER: a globular ornament of three-petalled flowers enclosing small balls.

BALUSTER: a small pillar or column, supporting a rail or coping.

BALUSTRADE: a series of balusters supporting a rail or coping.

BARGEBOARD: a barge is the overhanging edge of a roof up the slope of a gable and the board, usually decoratively carved, masks and protects the ends of the horizontal roof timbers.

BAROQUE: term applied to style of architecture, painting and sculpture, primarily associated with seventeenth-century Italy. English baroque is c.1692–1720, e.g. Hawksmoor, Vanbrugh.

BATTEN: a strip of wood, used for attaching slates and tiles to a roof or wall.

BATTLEMENT: an indented parapet, used on churches for decorative effect.

BAY: a division of a building, inside or outside, marked not by walls but units of vaulting, arches, roof compartments or windows.

BOSS: an ornamental projection used to conceal the intersection of ribs in a vault, or beams in a wooden ceiling.

BRACE: see ROOF.

BRACKET: a projection designed as a support.

BROACH: see SPIRE.

BUTTRESS: masonry, or brickwork, built against a wall to provide stability or to counteract the outward thrust of an arch or vault. FLYING BUTTRESS: an arch carrying thrust of vault or roof from walls to an outer pier or buttress.

CABLE: a convex moulding resembling a cable or rope.

CAMBER: slight rise or upward curve of an otherwise horizontal structure.

CANOPY: projection or hood over niche, pulpit, altar, sedilia, statue, etc.

CAPITAL: the top part of a column (or pilaster).

CARTOUCHE: a tablet set in an ornate frame or scroll.

CARYATID: a column in the form of a sculptured female figure.

CASEMENT: a window hinged on one side, opening outwards or inwards.

CASTELLATED: decorated like a castle with turrets and battlements.

CHAMFER: a flat splayed edge between two flat plain surfaces.

CHANCEL: part of the east end of a church where the altar is to be found, sometimes separated from nave by a screen.

CHANTRY CHAPEL: chapel within a church endowed for the saying of masses for the founder; often enclosed by screens.

CHEVET: circular or polygonal apse at east end of church, surrounded by ambulatory or radiating chapels.

CHEVRON: a zigzag form of ornamentation.

CHOIR: part of church where services are sung.

CLADDING: thin slabs of stone or other material used externally as a covering to the structure of a building.

CLASSICAL: style inspired by ancient Greece and Rome or by classical trends in Renaissance Europe.

CLERESTORY: the upper part of the nave, choir and transepts, containing a series of windows.

CLOISTER: covered walk around open space, usually square, with a plain wall on one side and piers or columns, sometimes with tracery, on the other. Attached to monasteries, often on south side of the church.

COLLAR: see ROOF.

COLONNADE: a row of columns supporting an entablature.

COPING: the capping of a wall to give weather protection.

CORBEL: a block of stone or piece of brickwork projecting from a wall to support a floor, roof, vault, parapet or other feature.

CORINTHIAN: see ORDERS.

CORNICE: topmost part of an entablature, and also any moulded projection which crowns the part to which it is fixed.

COURSE: a continuous layer of stone or brick of uniform height.

CRENELLATE: to fortify a residence with battlements and parapet.

CREST: line of ornament finishing a roof, wall, screen, etc.

CROCKET: ornament, usually in the form of buds or curled leaves, placed on the sloping sides of spires, gables, canopies and pinnacles.

CRUCK: a section of a curved tree split so that the two sections, one placed in reverse, formed a rough arch.

CRYPT: space below ground usually at east end of a church, sometimes called undercroft.

CUPOLA: small polygonal or circular domed turret on top of a roof.

CURTAIN WALL: outer wall of a castle.

DAUB: *see* WATTLE.

DECORATED: English Gothic architecture (*c.*1290–1360) characterized by tracery, at first geometric, then flowing.

DENTILS: small rectangular tooth-like blocks under a cornice.

DIAPER: an all-over pattern usually of lozenge, square or diamond shapes.

DOGTOOTH: a repeating ornament of four raised tooth-like pieces, usually set in a hollow moulding.

DOME: convex, hemispherical or semi-elliptical covering over a circular or polygonal space.

DORIC: *see* ORDERS.

DORMER: a window projecting vertically from a sloping roof.

DRESSING: refinements of worked and finished stones – e.g. architraves, keystones, quoins etc.

DRIPMOULD, DRIPSTONE: a projecting moulding over the heads of doorways and windows to throw off rain. *see* HOOD-MOULD.

EARLY ENGLISH: English Gothic architecture, broadly covering the thirteenth century.

EAVES: horizontal overhang of a roof beyond a wall.

ELEVATION: external face(s) of a building.

EMBATTLE: furnish with battlements.

FAÇADE: front of a building, particularly principal front.

FANLIGHT: semicircular, fan-shaped or rectangular window above door.

FAN VAULT: *see* VAULT.

FASCIA: name board over a shop window; horizontal division of an architrave; flat board covering ends of roof rafters under the eaves.

FENESTRATION: the arrangement of windows in a building.

FINIAL: the topmost feature, generally ornamental, of a gable, roof, pinnacle, or canopy.

FLUTED: vertical grooves, regular and concave, on a column.

FOLLY: an eye-catcher, a fantastic structure, sometimes deliberately ruinous, an architectural joke.

FOUR-CENTRED ARCH: a depressed, pointed arch of the Tudor period.

FREESTONE: stone of sufficiently fine grain to be cut 'freely' in any direction, with saw, mallet or chisel.

FRIEZE: part of the entablature between architrave and cornice.

GABLE: triangular portion of wall at the end of a ridge roof: a *Dutch gable* is curved and shaped and surmounted by a pediment; a *stepped gable* has stepped sides.

GALLERY: a long room or 'long gallery' usually on upper floor extending the length of a house; upper storey in a church, supported on columns above aisles.

GARGOYLE: a carved grotesque human or animal head serving as a spout from the top of a wall to throw off rainwater.

GAZEBO: look-out or elevated summer-house which commands a view.

GEOMETRIC TRACERY: tracery of simple geometric shapes e.g. circles and trefoils.

GIBBS SURROUND: window or door with keystoned head (three or sometimes five) under a cornice with a surround of stone blocks, alternating large and small, boldly punctuating jambs. So called after James Gibbs.

GLAZING BARS: strips of wood enclosing panes of glass in a window.

GOTHIC: style of architecture in England spanning the thirteenth to fifteenth centuries; divided chronologically into Early English, Decorated, and Perpendicular.

GOTHICK: the recreation and reinterpretation of English Gothic architecture in the eighteenth century.

GROTESQUE: decoration in the shape of fantastic animals, monsters, dragons etc., also human forms, flowers, fruit, etc.

HALLENKIRCHE, HALLCHURCH: church in which nave and aisles are of equal height.

HIP, HIPPED: *see* ROOF.

HOOD-MOULD: projecting moulding over an opening to throw off rain-water. *See* DRIPSTONE.

IONIC: *see* ORDERS.

JAMB: the vertical side of an archway, doorway or window.

JETTY: the overhang of an upper floor on a timber-framed building.

KEYSTONE: central stone of an arch or a ribbed vault.

KINGPOST: *see* ROOF.

LANCET: a narrow window terminating in a sharp point.

LANTERN: a small circular or polygonal turret with windows all round, crowning a roof or dome.

LIERNE RIBS: short subsidiary ribs tying main ribs in a vault. LIERNE-VAULT: *see* VAULT.

LIGHT: the division of a window by mullion and transom; can be further subdivided into panes.

LINENFOLD: panelling carved to look like vertically folded linen.

LINTEL: block of stone spanning top of a doorway or window.

LONG-AND-SHORT-WORK: Quoins, where flat horizontal stone slabs alternate with tall vertical ones, in Saxon building.

LOZENGE: diamond shape.

MANSARD: *see* ROOF.

MEDALLION: round or oval plaque bearing painted or carved figure.

METOPE: in Doric order of classical architecture, the space in the frieze between triglyphs.

MISERICORD: a bracket on the underside of a hinged wooden seat in a choir-stall which afforded support during long periods of standing.

MODILLION: small projecting brackets, often placed in a series below a classical cornice.

MOUCHETTE: curved dagger motif in tracery, popular in early fourteenth century.

MOULD, MOULDINGS: varieties of contour given to piers, arches etc. *See* CABLE, DOGTOOTH, DRIPSTONE.

MULLION: a vertical structural member subdividing a window.

NAVE: main body or central aisle of a church.

NICHE: a shaped recess in a wall or screen.

OBELISK: lofty, four-sided tapering shaft with pyramidal cap.

ŒIL-DE-BŒUF: round or oval window with glazing bars radiating from centre.

OGEE: a continuous double curve, concave above and convex below, or vice versa.

OOLITE: limestone mainly composed of abundant small calcareous grains, resembling the roe of a fish.

ORDERS: the classical styles of columns with combinations of base, shaft, capital and entablature; Doric (Greek, Roman and Tuscan), Ionic and Corinthian.

ORIEL: a window usually projecting from an upper storey.

OVERHANG: projecting upper storey of a building. *See* JETTY.

OVERTHROW: the fixed panel or arch, often elaborately decorated, above a wrought-iron gate.

PALLADIO, ANDREA: Italian architect (1508–80) whose work was introduced to England by Inigo Jones in 1615. It was revived in the eighteenth century by Colen Campbell and Lord Burlington. Hence 'Palladian'.

PANEL (TRACERY): where mullions run to the height of the arch and the tracery is of straight-sided vertical panels above the window lights.

PARAPET: a low wall on bridge, castle, church, gallery or balcony, above the cornice.

PARCLOSE: a screen separating a chapel or aisle from the body of the church.

PARTERRE: a flower-garden.

PEDIMENT: in classical, Renaissance and neo-classical buildings, a gable of low pitch, straight-sided or curved segmentally, above a door, window or portico.

PENDANT: elongated boss, projecting down or suspended from a fan vault, or ceiling.

PERPENDICULAR: period of English Gothic architecture *c.*1335–1530, characterized by strong vertical tracery.

PIANO NOBILE: the principal storey of a house containing the state rooms; usually the first floor.

PIER: a solid masonry support to sustain vertical pressure; simple – round, square or rectangular, or compound – composite and multiform, with mouldings and shafts.

PILASTER: a flat pier or shallow projection attached to a wall, with a base and capital.

PINNACLE: an ornament, pyramidical or conical and often decorated, which surmounts a gable or buttress.

PISCINA: a recess containing a shallow stone basin, with a drain, for washing sacred vessels, almost always to the south of an altar.

PLINTH: the projecting base of a wall or column, usually moulded or chamfered at the top.

POINTING: filling in the joint-lines of brick and stonework with mortar or cement, smoothed with the point of a trowel.

PORTICO: a covered colonnade providing an entrance to a building.

PULPIT: raised and enclosed area, of wood or stone, for a preacher. A three-decker consists of clerk's seat and reading-desk below, and the pulpit often has above it a tester, or flat canopy, serving as a sounding-board.

PURLIN: a longitudinal horizontal beam or pole supporting the common rafters of a roof.

QUOIN: a dressed stone at the external angle of a wall.

RAFTER: *see* ROOF.

RAGSTONE: a hard rubbly or coarse shelly stone.

RANDOM: not laid in courses; undressed stone of many shapes and sizes.

REBUS: visual pun, play on a name or words.

RENDERING: covering of an outer wall, with, for example, plaster, or cement and sand.

REREDOS: wall or screen behind an altar, usually ornamented.

RETICULATED TRACERY: tracery of net-like character.

RIB: a length of stone or wood, generally moulded, dividing the compartments of a vault or roof.

RIDGE: *see* ROOF.

ROCOCO: a decorative phase, in England *c.*1720–1760, especially associated with elaborately designed plasterwork, chimney-pieces and furniture.

ROLL: a plain moulding.

ROMANESQUE: style of architecture prevalent in the eleventh and twelfth centuries.

ROOD: a crucifix; the cross usually found in a Rood Loft, a gallery built over the rood screen.

ROOF:

[i] BRACE: an inclined timber, straight or curved, usually at an angle, introduced to strengthen others.

ROOF (*cont.*)

[ii] COLLAR: tie-beam (*see below*) applied higher up slope of roof.

[iii] HAMMERBEAM: a short beam projecting horizontally from top of wall but not meeting its corresponding member on the other side.

[iv] HIP: roof with sloped not vertical ends.

[v] KINGPOST: upright timber linking tie-beam and collar-beam with ridge-beam.

[vi] MANSARD: a roof with two pitches on each side of the ridge, the lower steeper than the other.

[vii] RAFTER: timbers sloping up from the bottom of the roof to the ridge at the top.

[viii] RIDGE: beam laid along apex of a roof which is met by upper ends of rafters.

[ix] SADDLEBACK ROOF: roof of a tower shaped like gabled timber roof.

[x] TIE-BEAM: beam connecting the upper surfaces of a solid wall or the post-heads of a timber-framed wall. May also form part of roof, e.g. when supporting a crown post.

[xi] TRUSS: a group of strong timbers arranged as a supporting frame within the triangle formed by the sloping sides of a timber-framed roof.

[xii] WAGON ROOF: a curved wooden rafter roof giving the appearance of the inside of a canvas tilt over a wagon.

[xiii] WIND-BRACE: diagonal braces crossing rafters to strengthen construction longitudinally.

ROSE-WINDOW: circular window with radiating or concentric tracery.

ROSETTE: carved ornament, painted or moulded, resembling a rose.

ROTUNDA: circular or oval building, often domed.

ROUNDEL: panel, disc or medallion, circular in shape.

RUBBLE, RUBBLESTONE: unsquared and undressed stone, not laid in regular courses.

RUSTICATION: the practice of surrounding blocks of stone by sunk joints in order to produce shadows.

SACRISTY: a room in or attached to a church where sacred vessels are kept.

SADDLEBACK: see ROOF.

SANCTUARY: area of a church around the main altar.

SASH: a glazed wooden frame which slides up and down by means of pulleys.

SCALLOPED CAPITAL: where the semicircular surface of the capital is elaborated into 'scallops' or a series of truncated cones.

SCREEN: *Parclose screen.* A partition separating a side chapel from rest of church. *Rood screen.* A screen below rood (*see* ROOD) generally at west end of chancel.

SEDILE (pl. *Sedilia*): seat or seats, usually three for the clergy on the south side of the chancel.

SEGMENT, SEGMENTAL: in an arch the segment of a semicircle drawn from a centre below the springing line.

SOLAR: parlour or private living-room, usually situated above undercroft, in a medieval house.

SPANDREL: the space, approximately triangular, between the outer curve of an arch and the rectangle formed by the mouldings enclosing it.

SPIRE: tall pyramidal or conical, tapering structure erected on top of a tower or roof. The diminutive is SPIRELET. *Broach spire.* An octagonal spire erected on a square tower.

SPROCKET: a short length of timber attached to the face of a rafter a little above the eaves in order to give the lowest part of a roof a flatter pitch.

STAGE: 'storey' of a tower, usually marked by a STRING COURSE.

STIFF-LEAF: foliage of conventional form, with stiff stems and lobed leaves that characterizes Early English ornament on mouldings etc.

STRAPWORK: sixteenth- and seventeenth-century flat interlaced decoration, seemingly derived from bands of cut leather.

STREY: transverse portion(s) or 'transept' of a medieval or tithe barn.

STRING COURSE: a moulding or narrow projecting course running horizontally along the face of a building.

STUCCO: plaster or external rendering, usually of a brick or rubblestone wall.

SWAG: an ornamental wreath or festoon of flowers, foliage or fruit fastened at both ends, and hanging down in the centre.

TEMPIETTO: a small, temple-like structure or shape.

TERMINAL: the upper part of a human figure growing out of pedestal, pier or pilaster which tapers towards its base.

TESSERAE: small blocks of marble, stone, etc. forming a mosaic.

TESTER: flat canopy serving as a sounding-board over a pulpit.

THREE-DECKER: *see* PULPIT.

TIMBER-FRAME: a wooden construction where walls and partitions are made as a timber framework, and filled in with plaster, wattle, daub, brick etc.

TIE-BEAM: *see* ROOF.

TRACERY: intersecting ornamental ribwork in the upper parts of Gothic windows, walls, screens and vaults.

TRANSEPT: an arm of the cross-piece of a cruciform church.

TRANSITIONAL: in-between stage between any two consecutive architectural styles, usually referring to the period between Norman and Early English.

TRANSOM: a horizontal structural member subdividing a window.

TREFOIL: a three-lobed or leaf-shaped arc in tracery separated by cusps.

TRIFORIUM: an arcaded wall passage or area of blank arcading above the main arcade of a church and below the clerestory.

TRIGLYPH: rectangular blocks with vertical grooves (glyphs) separating the METOPES in the Doric frieze.

TROMPE L'ŒIL: a painting giving the illusion that objects represented are real.

TRUSS: *see* ROOF.

TURRET: small round or polygonal tower.

TUSCAN: *see* ORDERS.

TYMPANUM: the area between the lintel and the arch of a doorway, often filled with relief sculpture.

UNDERCROFT: a vaulted room, sometimes underground, below another room.

VALLEY: the sloping junction of two inclined roof surfaces.

VAULT: arched roof of stone; *fan vault* where the length and curvature of the ribs which spring from the same point are similar; a *lierne vault* incorporates decorative short subsidiary ribs.

VENETIAN WINDOW: a window with three openings, the middle one arched and wider than the others.

VERNACULAR: local style of architecture, particularly associated with cottages, small houses and farm buildings in local building materials.

VESICA: pointed oval shape which, when it frames the figure of Christ, is called a mandorla or aureole.

VESTIBULE: an ante-room or entrance hall or passage.

VOUSSOIR: a wedge-shaped stone for an arch.

WAGON ROOF: *see* ROOF.

WATTLE: the infill between the elements of a timber-frame wall, made of interwoven sticks, staves, twigs, laths, as a backing for DAUB, a rough plastering over with mud or clay.

WIND-BRACE: *see* ROOF.

ZIGZAG: chevron or zigzag moulding or decoration characteristic of Norman (Romanesque) architecture.

Index

Descriptions of towns and villages in the text are arranged in alphabetical order, and are not listed here. This index, *inter alia*, is intended to point more to subject matter, building materials, architects and artists, designers and craftsmen, supplementary place names, and some bibliographical, geographical and historical references. Page numbers of photographs are shown in **bold type**

Naunton, 113, 138; Painswick, 8, 148; Poulton, 154; Quarry Hill, Bibury, 20, 22, 26; Slaughter, 138; Stonesfield, 8, 42, 89, 135, 138 154, 174; Stumps Cross, 171; Taynton, 8, 14, 22, 124, 165, 180; Tolldown, 103; Westington, 65; Windrush, 195

Queen Anne buildings, 29, 30, **32**, 53, **55**, 82, 84, 133

Radcliffe Camera, Library, 184
rectories, 9, 29, 42, **46**, 48, 88, 94, 123, **123**, 140, 145, 155, 190, 198
Redesdale, Lord, 180, 190
Redundant Churches Fund, 92
Regency buildings, 23, 159–60
Rendcomb, Gloucestershire, 10, 168
Repton, G. S., 68
Repton, Humphrey, 68, 160
Reynolds, Sir Joshua, 206
ribbon-pointing of stone, 53, 139
Ricardo, David, MP, 133
Rice, D. Talbot, 159
Rickman, Thomas, 117–18, 187
Rochdale, Lancashire, 198
Romans, 9–10, 71; Chedworth, 58–9; Cirencester, (Corinium), 71; Cornovii, 71; Emperor Diocletian, 71; Woodchester, 204
Rossetti, Dante Gabriel, 119–20, 158
roughcast, 13, 100, 104, 125, 139
Russell, Gordon, 38, 40, 143
Rysbrack, J. M., 114, 160, 184

Salvin, Anthony, 160
St Aubyn, J. P., 167
St George's Chapel, Windsor, 114
St John's College, Oxford, 23
St Martin-in-the-Fields, London, 114, 206
St Paul's Cathedral, London, 23
Saxon architecture, 10, 15, 17, 25, 26, 88, 90, **90**, 91, **91**
Scheemakers, Henry, 133
Schrider, Christopher, 206
Scott, Sir George Gilbert, 14, 17, 119, 176, 192, 194
Scott, Sir Philip, 170
Seymour, Sir Thomas, 175
Shakespeare, William, 135n
Shapland, W. T. Carter, 106
Sheldon, Ralph, 57
Sheldonian Theatre, Oxford, 23
Shelley, Percy Bysshe, 124
Sherwood, Jennifer, 50n, 57
Simmons, Jack, 7, 74n
Sitwell, Sacheverell, 114
Slad, Painswick, 148
Smith, A. E., 200
Smith, Francis, 'of Warwick', 48, 184
Smythson, Robert, 57, 148
Society for the Protection of Ancient Buildings, 50, 118, 119, 144
Souillac, Lot, France, 127
Southwell Minster, Nottinghamshire, 28
Spence, Basil, 142
St John's College, Cambridge, 118, 187
stained glass, other than Victorian, 10, 34, 44, 49, 65,

74, 106, 109–10, **111**(2), 115, **115**, 116, 119, 136, 139, 142, 144, 156, 170, 176, *see also* Victorian
Steane, John M., *Investigations at Cogges*, 85n
Stone, Nicholas, 65, 160
Stonesfield, Oxfordshire, stone roofing slates, 8, 42, 89, 135, 138, 154, 174
Street, G. E., 10, 35, 50, 85, 113, 117, 164, 187, 203
Strong, Roy, 20n
Strong, Edward, 22; Thomas, 23, 25; Timothy, 165; Valentine, 160, 165
Stuart buildings, other than Queen Anne, **12**, 13, 19, **19**, 25–6, 29, **30**, 38, 41, **46**, 47, **47**, 48, **49**, 57–8, 62, 63, **63**, **64**, 76, **102**, 103–4, 117, **118**, 123, **123**, 132–3, **132**, 140, 163, 170, 172, **172**, **173**, 174, 193, **194**, 205
stucco, 19, 85, 112
Sumsion, Thomas, 96
Sylvester, family tombs, 49

Talman, William, 103
Teulson, S. S., 147, 204
Tewkesbury Abbey, Gloucestershire, 50, 115, 119
thatch, 14, 34, 89, 120, 135
timber-frame, 18, 45, 76, 80, 135, 150, 175, 184
tithe barns, 14, 29
Toledo cathedral, Spain, 190
Tolstoy, Leo, 138
tomb-chests, 10, 26, 60, 134, 143, 148, 150, **151**, 155, 159, 167, 168, 190, 197, 204
tufa, 96
tympanum-a, 24, 35, 60, 88, 94, 104, 105–6, **105**, 128, 139, 155, 160, 177(2), 190

Vanbrugh, Sir John, 68, 103
Vaughan-Williams, Ralph, 157
Verey, David, 7, 25, 28, 29, 109, 132, 139, 165n
Verey, Mrs D. C. W., 20
Versailles, Palace of, France, 103
vicarages, 9, 13, 47, **47**, 50–1, 85–6, **85**, 125, 151, **152**, 166(2), 167, 169
Victoria Museum, Calcutta, 160
Victorian buildings; 10, 19, 33, 66, 68, **69**, 82, 113, 147, 158, 159, 164, 165, 175, 187, **189**, 194, 204, 205; glass, 15, 35, 36, 49, 54, 68, 96, 112, 124, 143, 158–9, 169, 175, 177, 187, 193, 203, 206; restorations, 14, 17, 19, 20, 24, 25, 36, 42, 50, 51, 85, 96, 117, 121, 131, 136, 143, 148, 163, 165, 167, 175, 176–7, 194, 195, 197, 203
Viollet-le-Duc, E. E., 204
Vulliamy, Lewis, 25, 147

Wailes, 112
Waller, F. S., 124, 155; and Son, 138
wall painting, 10, 17, 25, 29, 46, 52, **52**, 116, 117, 119, 120, 144–5, 177
Walpole, Horace, 134
Warren, 30
Warwick, 48; Beauchamp Chapel, St Mary, 34
Webb, Christopher, 142
Webb, Geoffrey, 163
Webb, John, 162
Webb, Philip, 35, 120